Fort Collins

· A HISTORY ·

BARBARA FLEMING

THE History PRESS

Published by The History Press
Charleston, SC 29403
www.historypress.net

First published 2014

Manufactured in the United States

ISBN 978.1.62619.725.1

Library of Congress Cataloging-in-Publication Data

Fleming, Barbara Allbrandt, 1936-
Fort Collins : a history / Barbara Fleming.
pages cm
Summary: "Explore the fascinating history of Fort Collins"-- Provided by publisher.
Includes bibliographical references and index.
ISBN 978-1-62619-725-1 (paperback)
1. Fort Collins (Colo.)--History. 2. Fort Collins (Colo.)--Biography. I. Title.
F784.F56F545 2014
978.8'68--dc23
2014036946

This book is dedicated to the undaunted early settlers who came to the Poudre Valley and decided to invest their faith, and their futures, in Fort Collins.

Contents

Acknowledgements

Writing is lonely work, but putting together a book like this requires a coterie of individuals who help guide it through the various stages of creation and production. My immense gratitude, once again, to local history archivist Lesley Drayton and her assistant, Jayne Hansen, for their continued help with images and to my friend and co-author Malcolm McNeill for his books, the Barney letters and his photographs and postcards. My thanks as well to Laurie D'Aubney of Fort Collins Utilities, who graciously provided images; to Barbara Moore, who graciously shared her art with me again; to Patrick Clements, who took pictures; to Danny Rogers, who shared Cunningham images; and to participants in my Front Range Forum history class, from whom I gleaned details to enrich this book. I am very grateful to my editor, Becky LeJeune, who has been enormously helpful throughout the process. So many books have been written about this town, so many resources are available, but any errors are my own. The majority of photographs come from the local history archive unless otherwise indicated. Each archive caption is followed by an identification number.

Introduction

Beginning as a military outpost in the early years of the westward expansion, Fort Collins, Colorado, was favored with a temperate climate featuring many days of sunshine, intensely blue skies, a river flowing through a lushly vegetated valley, abundant wildlife, imposing hills to the west and clear air. It is not surprising that the small settlement that started here in the late 1860s drew more settlers. Commerce helped the community to thrive, and in due time, the town acquired a land grant college and a railroad.

Today, few traces of the town's beginnings remain. A thriving city of more than 150,000 people featuring the sprawling campus of a large university, Fort Collins has become a diverse place that has attracted retirees, enticed students to stay around after they graduate and provided appealing conditions for business and industry.

Not that the course of history has been smooth for this town. Its people have been battered by fires, blizzards and floods; tested by drought and hordes of flying insects; and deeply affected by distant wars. They have struggled with issues of discrimination and lived through economic downturns. Yet those who chose to live here in the beginning persisted through the dark days; those who came later and were set back by adversity got right up again and persevered. Through strong differences of opinion and years of prohibition, the townspeople have worked to create a community in which people want to live.

The small town Fort Collins once was, the small town in which I grew up, has faded into history. Fortunately for that history, many people here have taken and continue to take an interest in our colorful past, enough interest to help preserve the charming downtown area I remember so well. The business establishments have changed, of course, but most of the buildings are much the same. Our downtown is a lively, bustling place where one will nearly always find shoppers strolling around and events going on.

When I grew up here in the 1940s, the town extended about a mile or two in each direction, easily walked from one end to the other. The campus center was an oval with green grass that had a tree-lined lane in the middle of it, with only a few buildings beyond. One of them was Old Main, the first classroom building and home to the college's first president. I went to small neighborhood grocery stores where credit was extended to children of families known to shop there, saw movies at two theaters on College and Mountain Avenues, rode a trolley to City Park and went to school in an old brick building constructed before the turn of the century. That town lives only in memory now. What a wonderful place it was to grow up!

This book offers an overview of how Fort Collins came to be what it is today, looking at the time before the arrival of settlers, the establishment of the military camp followed by the birth of the town, the later decades of the nineteenth century and the enormous changes the new century brought and the evolution of a small town into a mid-sized city. The history of this town is rich and colorful, full of stories both lively and sad. History is the stories of the people who lived it; the people who decided to settle here have left for us many tales that stand the test of time. It is my pleasure to share these stories with you.

Chapter 1

In the Valley

Before

A lush river valley, teeming with wildlife, carpeted by vegetation, framed to the west by rugged foothills and high peaks beyond—that's what young Antoine Janis saw when he came to the Poudre River Valley in 1842. Antoine came with his father to trap animals for fur. Trappers and the Native Americans who roamed the land were then the only inhabitants, and they were always on the move. The two groups respected each other and gave each other space, so Papa Janis felt unthreatened in bringing his teenage son with him on that expedition. As for Antoine, he was enchanted and dubbed the valley "the loveliest spot on earth."

The legend of the river's name, *Cache la Poudre* (French for, loosely, "where the powder is hidden"), is hazy. The most enduring story is that French trappers would sometimes cache, or hide, gunpowder and other supplies along the riverbank. If found by another trapper or a soldier, the cache would typically be left undisturbed. Who buried powder, and where, is uncertain, for there are several stories, but it is highly probable, according to historian John Gray, that the river had its name by about 1835. So it would have been known as such to young Antoine.

In 1843, close to the same time that Antoine Janis first visited the Poudre Valley, famed explorer John Charles Fremont led an expedition up the rugged Poudre Canyon. Only the wild river, with its roiling, rushing water, made a path through the dense forest of aspen and pine trees, along with various kinds of native shrubs. Towering peaks rose above the men to their

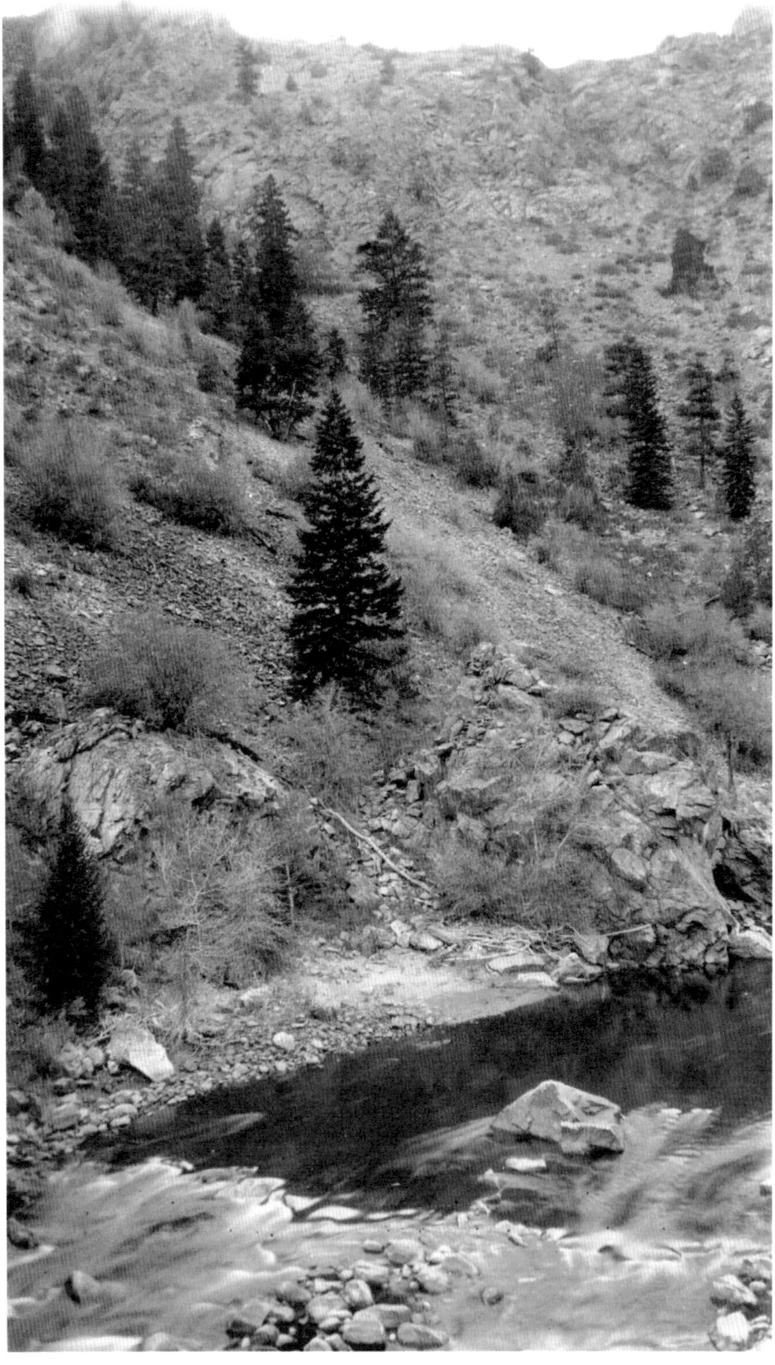

Wild, formidable Poudre Canyon was carved by the Cache la Poudre River eons before humans arrived here and looked much like this when they first came. *H24216.*

right and left. Wild animals, including bears and mountain lions, roamed the area. Fremont later recorded that they had to fight for every foot of ground as they sought the headwaters of the mighty river. At last, weary, footsore and defeated, Fremont called off the expedition and turned his men back toward the North Platte River, their starting place. A local legend says that Stove Prairie, a small settled area in Rist Canyon west of Fort Collins, got its name because the Fremont expedition abandoned a lightweight cooking stove there on their way back.

Fremont was to lead several more expeditions more successful than that one, and he eventually gained national attention when he ran for president, unsuccessfully, in 1856. But he failed to complete the Poudre Canyon exploration, although he wrote vivid descriptions of the area. Successfully navigating the canyon was left to others, who were to come later. Today, it is hard to imagine that the now tamed canyon, with its paved road and many dwellings, was once too rugged to penetrate.

Other explorers had preceded Fremont. Among those known to have been here are William Ashley, a trapper who founded the Rocky Mountain Fur Company, and Richens Wooten, a trader. William Sublette, another trapper, worked for Ashley until he bought Ashley out. We do know that fur trappers and others had commerce with native people long before any eastern immigrants formed permanent settlements in the river valley. By the late 1840s, the mountain men and their roaming lifestyle were nearly gone. The Hudson Fur Company had crushed the smaller Rocky Mountain Company, and beaver hats had gone out of style. No doubt this was a good thing for the beaver, which might have become extinct had the trapping continued at its earlier frenetic pace.

Long, long before Janis and Fremont arrived in this area, a band of primitive people later labeled Folsom Man lived in an area north and west of Fort Collins known today as the Soapstone Prairie, a natural area owned and managed by the city. In the 1920s, Claude and A. Lynn Coffin, brothers and amateur archaeologists, found weapons, bones and other artifacts indicating that there had been a settlement in that area about twelve thousand years ago, most probably by people whose ancestors had migrated from Siberia over the land bridge. In the 1930s, the Smithsonian Institution sent archaeologists to explore the site. They found more than five thousand items, including spear points, proving that the men hunted buffalo, which were then abundant on the high plains. Folsom Man lived in the area for an indefinite amount of time, surviving on buffalo meat and other game.

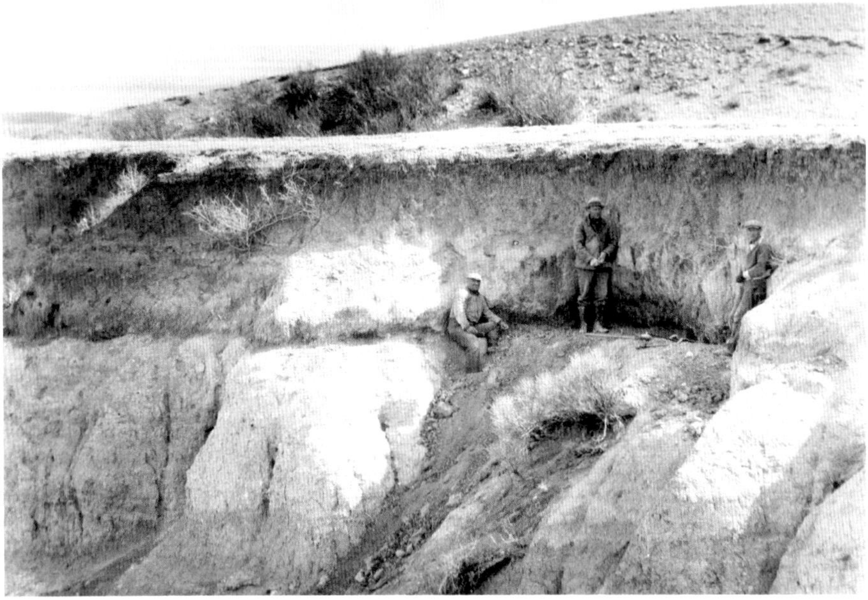

In the mid-1920s, Major Roy Coffin (left), his brother A. Lynn Coffin (right) and Judge Claude C. Coffin (center) discovered an archaeological site inhabited by Folsom Man about twelve thousand years ago. *Courtesy of Malcolm McNeill.*

The chronology following the Folsom habitation is fuzzy. Certainly, indigenous peoples roamed this area, hunting and fishing, for millennia. By the 1700s, Spanish explorers had come, mingling and sometimes warring with the Native American tribes inhabiting the area. The Spaniards brought horses, modern weapons and disease to America, in some places wiping out whole populations. One explorer, Don Pedro de Villasur, came here in 1720 seeking the French, who had reportedly armed some tribes. Villasur was killed near the Platte River, along with thirty-two of his soldiers, by hostile Pawnees.

France had owned the land for a time; France and Spain, not infrequently at war, had traded ownership of the American West since the continent was discovered by Europeans in the 1400s. Colorado, the name itself of Spanish origin, has many towns and counties named for the Spanish who came here, particularly in the southern part of the state, but few bearing French names.

In 1803, the territory belonged to France until it was sold by Napoleon Bonaparte as part of the Louisiana Purchase—resulting in the 1804–6 Lewis and Clark expedition that opened up the West. Their epic westward exploration confirmed the existence of thousands upon thousands of acres of open land and species of flora and fauna hitherto unknown, and it also spelled the beginning of the end for the free-ranging Native Americans who had populated the land for so long.

Westward migrations did not begin on a mammoth scale until several decades later, but more explorers came, along with mountain men living by their skill and wits, all adding to what was known about the vast land now belonging to the United States of America. The people living in the more settled half of the country knew only that the land to the west was there. They knew that a backbone of mountains had to be crossed to reach the western coast; they knew that mighty rivers flowed through the land and that there were species of creatures never before heard of. In 1849, they learned that these lands contained riches to be had for the taking. Migration began en masse with the gold rush to California.

At that time, this valley was still unsettled, just a pass-through on the road to riches. By the next decade, change had come rather quickly. The small settlement of Laporte (meaning "door" or "gate"), which had begun earlier as a stopping place for traders and trappers, became a gateway for travelers headed from the south or east toward the Oregon Trail, which went through Wyoming. By 1860, a peaceable Arapaho tribe had set up camp at Laporte. Its chief, Friday Fitzpatrick, had become separated from his tribe when he was a boy and was found by Thomas Fitzpatrick, who took him in, named him and sent him to school, where he learned to speak English. Returning to his tribe as an adult, Friday was chosen as chief and often worked as an interpreter, since he was fluent in his native tongue and in English and not hostile toward the white man.

Sometimes, however, the tribes were hostile toward one another, different tribes fighting for the same hunting grounds. In the fall of 1858, as recorded later by Ansel Watrous in his book, a band of Arapahos, led by Chief Friday, did battle with a band of Pawnees who were on their annual buffalo hunt. Each occupying one side of a ridge north and west of what would become Fort Collins, the braves fought fiercely for three days straight. The Pawnees saw the Arapahos as trespassers on their territory and sought to drive them off. Knowing they would be tortured if captured, the Arapahos fought desperately for their lives. On the night of the third day, with both sides suffering wounded and dead and those still alive exhausted but determined, a "terrific mountain storm" gave the Pawnees cover to quietly depart. Friday, known among his people by his birth name, Warshinun (Black Spot), reported many of his fighters dead, in part because the Pawnees occupied the high

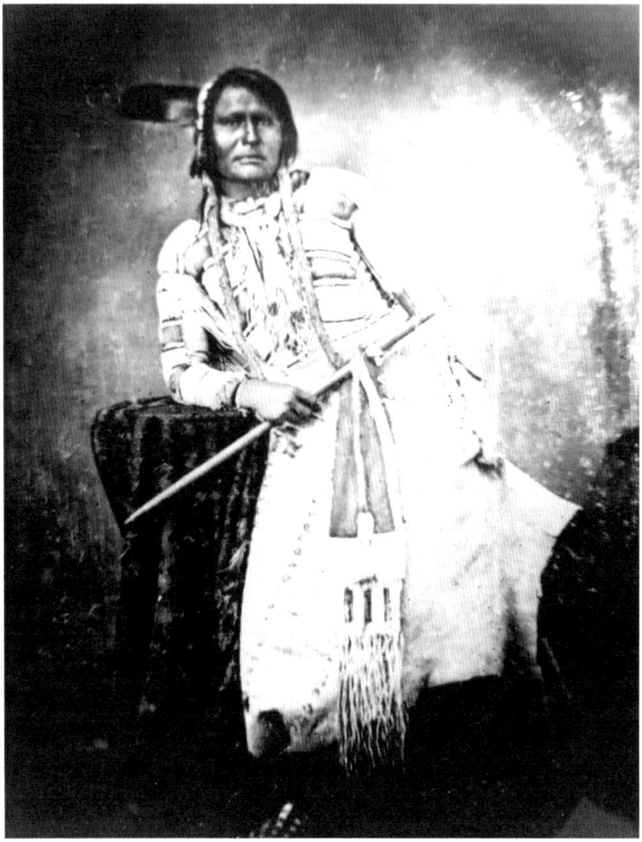

Raised among Anglos, Friday Fitzpatrick returned to his people as an adult and led his peaceable tribe even into confinement at the Wind River reservation in Wyoming in 1870. *H05383.*

ground and could shoot their arrows down at their foes. Watrous states that this was the last tribal battle fought in Larimer County.

Yet the natives resented the intruders. Watrous's book is peppered with accounts of encounters with hostile warriors in the late 1850s and early 1860s, especially after the start of the Civil War when it was evident to the tribes that the troops sent to contain them had been greatly depleted in numbers, giving them hope of keeping their lands.

Janis returned several years after his first visit as a boy, now a grown man planning to spend his days in the mountain west. Having good relations with the Oglala Lakota who often camped in the area, he soon took a bride, Elk Woman, and they began camping and trapping along the river. Before long, they had a family. In 1858, the Janis family came back to this area to settle down, and Antoine built what is considered the first dwelling in the valley designed for permanence. Janis, John B. Provost, Francis and Nicholas Janis, Antoine le Beau and Oliver Morrisette, along with a few others, founded a settlement in April 1859 and named it the Colona Town Company. Provost built a log house in the new town. By October 1860, the town had been reorganized as the Laporte Townsite Company. Residents marked off 1,280 acres on both sides of the river. The small community was designated the seat of Larimer County, territory of Colorado. (Colorado officially became a territory in 1861, upon which the territorial legislature created counties. Larimer County was named after William Larimer, considered the founder of Denver.) The first county administrators were Frederick Sherwood, Alfred Howes and John Ryan.

This settlement was rather casual; according to Gray, residents often left on long hunting trips, and few could be found when the census taker came in 1860.

That same year, a stage station was established at Laporte as a connection to the Overland Trail. Soon the town boasted saloons, a hotel, the county courthouse and jail, a very busy general store, blacksmith and livery shops and a brewery. It was the most important stage stop in Northern Colorado, conveying U.S. mail among other cargo—and passengers as well. (In his novel *Roughing It*, Mark Twain describes a stagecoach ride in graphic detail.)

One infamous, and perhaps maligned, stage station manager, Jack Slade, earned his place in history beginning with the murder of a grown man when Slade was only fourteen. He left home and joined the army, fighting in the Mexican-American War, and eventually came to Northern Colorado. Slade managed the station at Virginia Dale, which he had named after his wife, Virginia. The station, located near U.S. Highway 287 north of Fort Collins, has been preserved.

Virginia apparently managed to keep Slade sober most of the time; when not inebriated he was a good manager. However, he did not stay sober all the time and, when drunk, tended to wreak havoc. On one occasion, he did serious damage to the Laporte general store. After he sobered up, he paid reparations.

During a quarrel with Jules Beni, who lived and worked in northeastern Colorado (the town of Julesburg is named after him), Slade shot and killed his adversary and then cut off his ears, wearing them the rest of his life on his watch fob and earning him the fearsome reputation Twain wrote of in *Roughing It.* (Twain was grateful that he had escaped alive from a chance

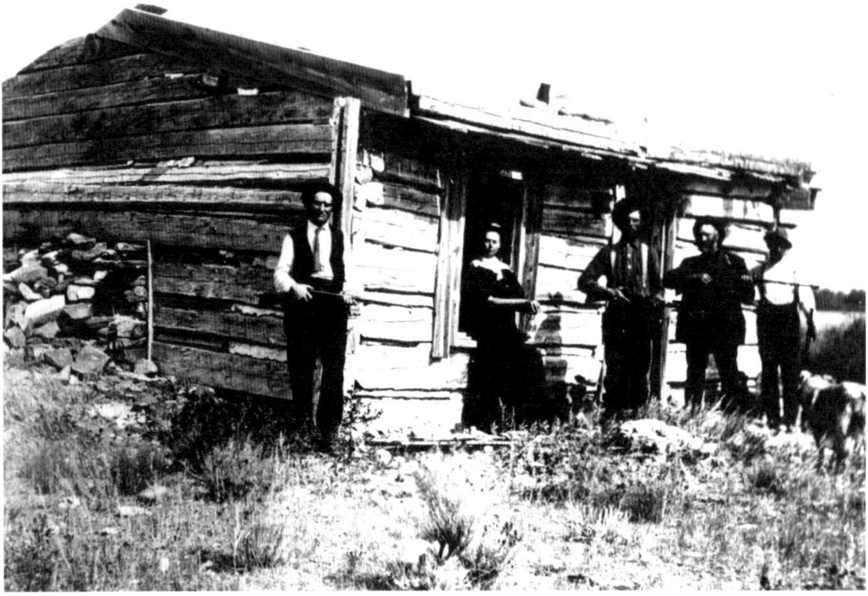

Shown at the far left casually leaning against the building, the notorious Jack Slade poses with his wife, Virginia, and other cowboy cohorts lounging in front of a crudely constructed log house. *H08139.*

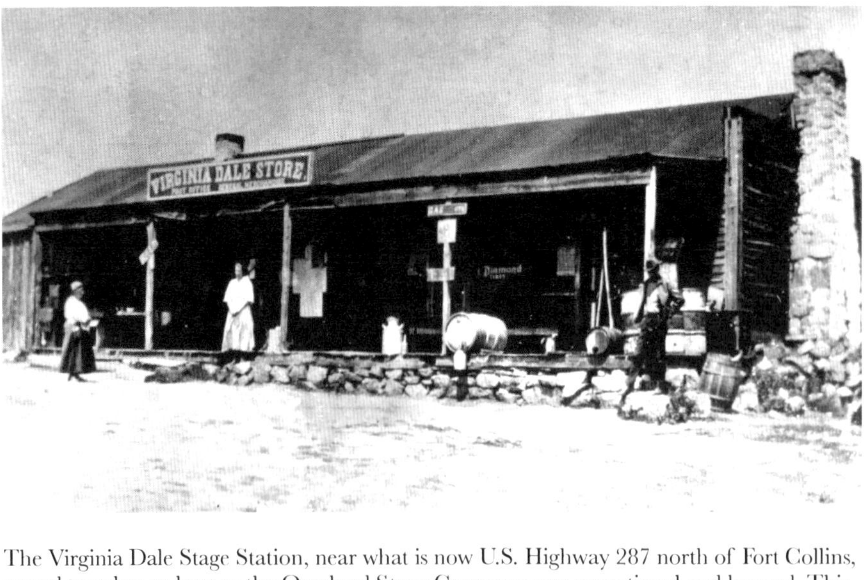

The Virginia Dale Stage Station, near what is now U.S. Highway 287 north of Fort Collins, served travelers as long as the Overland Stage Company was operational and beyond. This photograph was taken in 1916. *H08130.*

encounter with Slade.) Slade was not destined for a long life; in his early thirties, let go from the stage station job because of his drinking, he went to Montana, wreaked more havoc and was hanged by an angry group of citizens. Virginia rode desperately to save him but was too late. One Fort Collins resident, William Stover, witnessed the hanging and heard Slade cry, "My god, my god, must I die?"

Along with the Laporte stage station, a toll bridge (five to eight dollars to cross, depending on the size of the wagon) crossed the swift-flowing river. Travelers left the river at that point, turning north toward Wyoming more or less along the route of the present U.S. Highway 287. Ben Holladay, owner of the stage company, rerouted the trail after the start of the Civil War. The trail followed the Platte River west to the Poudre, which runs northwest to southeast, before turning north.

The Cherokee Trail, which joined the Overland Trail, originated in Oklahoma in the 1850s, when a group of once-prosperous Cherokees, whose forebears had been forced to leave their ancestral home and march on the deadly Trail of Tears, decided to strike out for California to find gold. Cherokees had successfully mined gold in Georgia until these proud people were driven off their land. They had the experience and expertise—why not go? So the first expedition joined forces with an Anglo group and headed north, seeking passage through the mountains across Wyoming—much easier than crossing the Rocky Mountains in Colorado. In time, the trail they forged became known as the Cherokee Trail. Some of the deep wagon ruts they made are still visible, including a faint trail near the old Fort Collins waterworks on Overland Trail. The Cherokee Trail continued northwest to the stage station at Virginia Dale and on into Wyoming to connect with the more widely used Overland Trail, which had been initially established as a mail route and soon was widely traversed as an alternative to the Oregon Trail.

In this day of modern transportation and conveniences, it is challenging to picture what these adventurers, lured westward by the promises of the Homestead Act of 1862 or dreams of gold, endured. Travel by wagon was slow, often delayed by the need to ford a stream, avoid a muddy area, find drinkable water or locate forage for the animals hauling the wagons. Any day that a wagon train made twenty-five miles was a very good one. The sun bore down on them; the canvas wagon covers were little protection against rain, hail and lightning. Storms could spook the animals. Much more feared than attacks by Native Americans were dry lands where no water ran except occasional salinated pools and no timber for fire could be gathered. They needed fire at night to ward off coyotes and other predators and to cook their food; they

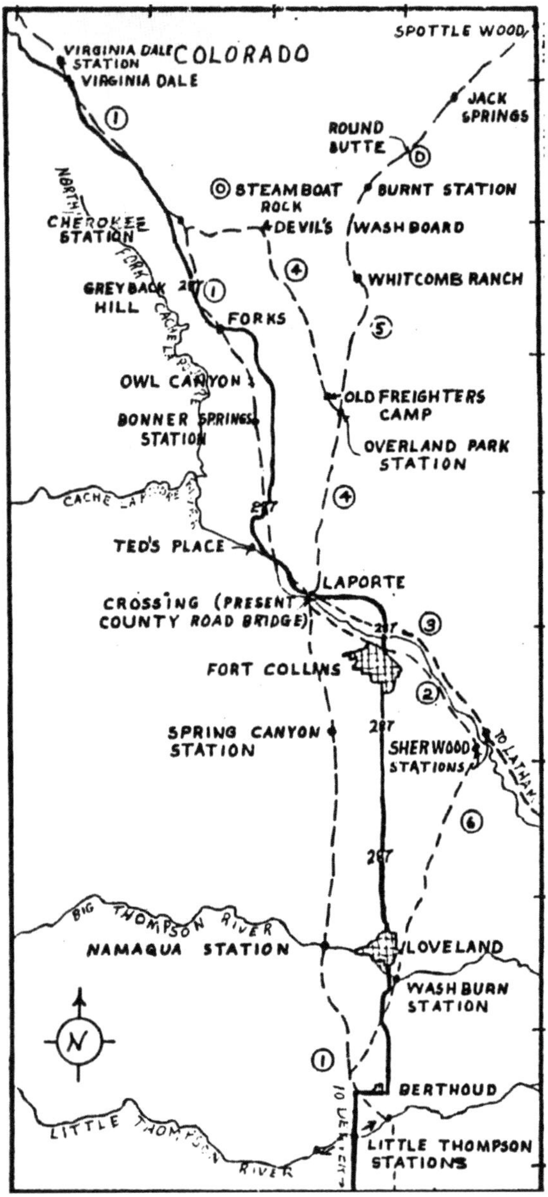

Richard Baker drew this map that shows the route of the Overland Stage Company toward the Virginia Dale stage station through Laporte. *H22178.*

needed water always and had to be wary of brackish or contaminated water. To lighten the loads, everyone who could walk did walk, wearing holes even in sturdy boots and shoes. Furniture and household goods, which had been loaded with such high hopes, were frequently abandoned along the trail. Walkers had to be on the lookout for rattlesnakes, prevalent in high, dry country, and for unexpectedly uneven ground or stones that could cause them to trip and sprain an ankle or break a bone.

Prairie fire was an ever-present danger, for there was nothing to stop it and limited means to fight it except by building berms over which it could not leap. And even though they knew the mountains were there, the sight of those towering peaks in the distance must have inspired dread rather than awe, for they had to be surmounted in order to reach California.

One can only wonder at the bravado of these travelers who left behind everything that was familiar and comfortable to venture into a vast unknown, only crudely mapped. They had no means of knowing what lay ahead, while behind them were family, neighbors, friends, conveniences and safety. Each day was a new challenge.

Once in a while, a few adventurous youths forsook the wagons and headed off on horseback, with a pack animal tethered behind. Like the emigrants, they needed to find shelter at night—not easy to come by in open areas—along with the basic needs: food, water and forage. They were tough, and the horses were tough, but these journeys asked of both man and beast the maximum effort and endurance they could put forth. Some of these men eventually joined the mountain men still living their solitary lives in the wilderness. Some, no doubt, did not live to tell their tales. A few may have become army scouts or guides.

Despite the stream of wagons heading for California, some of which stayed in this area, the Front Range in northern territorial Colorado remained relatively unpeopled until the 1860s. When the Civil War broke out, the Native Americans who had been vigorously resisting the intrusions on their hunting grounds took advantage of the small numbers of soldiers manning the forts to attack émigrés. More and more attacks were slowing the westward movement; people were dying and being captured by braves, sometimes tortured, so President Abraham Lincoln ordered that some troops be diverted from the war to protect travelers. Military posts were set up. One of these was Fort Laramie in northeastern Wyoming, commanded by Colonel William O. Collins.

Collins's Eleventh Ohio Cavalry had expectations of fighting for the Union. Instead, he and his troops were sent to Fort Laramie to protect pioneers along the Overland Trail, increasingly used not only by emigrants but also by supply trains, paymasters and, occasionally, VIPs. Soon, the Cherokee Trail, which passed near Laporte, was also experiencing significant harassment, so Collins was ordered to send troops to Laporte and set up an encampment. Camp Collins was put in place in July 1862. Here is where the story of Fort Collins begins.

Chapter 2

From Camp to Fort

Beginnings

Camp Collins was just that—a camp. There were few amenities, and few buildings were erected—only officers' quarters, a few cabins for the soldiers and stables for the horses. Some of the enlisted men lived in tents. The camp was placed near the town along the riverbank, where there was a ready source of clear water. Forage was all around them. The trading post supplied necessities. Trees growing near the river provided lumber and firewood. A blacksmith shop made sure their mounts were well shod. For a change from the everyday, there were the saloons in Laporte.

The camp, named after the popular Commander Collins, was commissioned on July 22, 1862, with the mission of protecting emigrant wagon trains. Although the nearby Arapahos and Cheyennes were not hostile (except that they did steal a horse or two from time to time), Plains Indians—Pawnees and Lakotas—were. A scare earlier in 1862 had particularly alarmed settlers when some Utes stole horses belonging to Jesse and Frederick Sherwood, who were farming southeast of the settlement. The brothers had come west in 1860 searching for gold and soon settled in the valley, raising cattle and horses and, for a time, hosting a stage station. Arapahos camped on their land; the Sherwoods were friendly with Native Americans.

But other settlers were anxious. Rumors flew; some people departed for safer climes.

Despite the settlers' concern about Native Americans on the warpath, the fort was not walled like the familiar stockades of western movie fame.

Initially, it was manned by the Ninth Kansas Cavalry, which was relieved by a Colorado volunteer cavalry; later, the First Colorado came. In mid-May, 1864, Company F of the Eleventh Ohio arrived. The commander was Captain William H. Evans.

Life at the camp was harsh. Like the emigrants venturing westward, the soldiers had to be tough. The high plains climate was typically dry in summer and bitter cold in winter. The fare was simple, basic. No entertainments and means of communications such as are available today were at hand for these troops. The soldier's most important companion was his horse. The value of his horse to the cavalry soldier cannot be overstated. Each man looked after his mount with great care; he depended on the animal to get him from one place to another and to hold steady during times of combat. Consequently, the horses had to be well fed and sheltered, brushed and curried daily. Saddles had to be carefully maintained. Rifles, too, were crucial and had to be cleaned regularly. So although entertainment opportunities were meager, the soldiers stayed busy enough. Frequently, units rode out to protect the stage line or travelers along the Cherokee Trail. Winter, summer, spring and fall, they wore the same heavy uniforms.

Evans was a by-the-book commander who insisted on strict discipline. Though they may have chafed at times under his command, the soldiers went about their daily routines as usual until the night of June 9, 1864. The winter of 1863 had produced, Watrous says, "a great body of snow," which, when it began to melt in the spring, filled the rivers and streams to overflowing. The Poudre River, usually well within its banks, could not on that night contain the amount of water pouring downstream. In the middle of the night, soldiers woke to find themselves in the midst of rushing water. Helpless, they watched everything wash away in the flood. They climbed onto rooftops and waited out the night. No one died, but the camp disappeared as though it had never been.

Evans decided it was time to move the camp to higher ground. He sent a message to Colonel Collins, who agreed that they should look for a new location. Accordingly, the captain sent Lieutenant James Hanna south along the river to look for a better spot.

A story told half a century later in a souvenir program survives to this day:

> *Captain Evans sent Lieutenant Hanna with a detail of troopers to look up a new location…On the homeward march, they fortunately met and fell in with Joseph Mason, who lived in a log cabin about a mile upstream from*

> *the present site of Fort Collins. Mr. Mason was one of the pioneers of the Cache la Poudre Valley, having settled here in 1860, and was familiar with this entire section of the country. He knew what the soldiers were looking for and met them before they reached his home. He pointed out to them the advantages and disadvantages of different locations along the river and finally persuaded them that they could find no better site in the valley for a military camp than that now occupied by the city of Fort Collins. It is strongly hinted that a well filled black bottle which Mr. Mason had in his coat pocket had much to do in convincing Hanna of the truth in Mr. Mason's contentions. If that was really true, there are not many, even in saloon-less Fort Collins, who would strenuously deny that there might be times when the contents of a black bottle, if they were of the right kind, possessed some virtue, as in this particular case they led to the founding of Fort Collins.*

True or not, it is a colorful story of Fort Collins's beginnings, especially given that the town was dry from the 1890s until the 1960s. Mason had made a claim near the land he recommended for the new fort, and he had plans to become the camp's sutler. (The term "sutler" referred to a civilian merchant who sold goods to soldiers.) It was high ground along the river, much less likely to flood, and it had a good view in every direction, which helped make it a safe spot for a military post. It also had good drainage. On August 20, 1864, Colonel Collins issued the official order for the new site, and Fort Collins was born.

Consider the camp site: We know with reasonable certainty that Old Grout, the building that served as the sutler's store and later as a hotel and jail, among other uses, stood more or less at the southwest corner of Jefferson and Linden Streets. We know, too, that in those days people did not think of these buildings as historic or worthy of preservation, only in terms of how useful they might be and whether they were impediments to growth. After the fort was abandoned it did not take long for all of the buildings on the site to disappear except Old Grout, which lasted a few more decades. Today, the only remaining reminder of the fort is Elizabeth Stone's cabin, now preserved in Library Park.

History is murky regarding how "Camp Collins" became "Fort Collins." Watrous claims that "fort" was chosen because it was more sophisticated than "camp." No one is certain, however, and references to Camp Collins could still be found after the move was made. Undoubtedly, the new site was more advantageous, no matter how it was known.

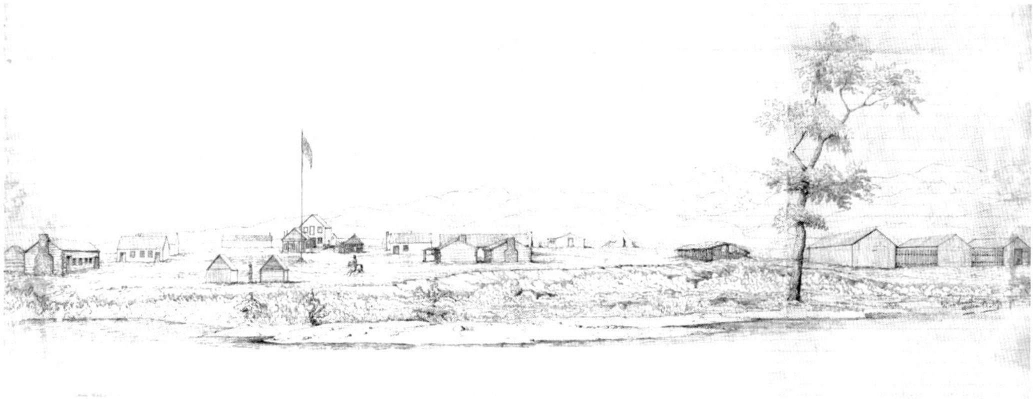

This drawing of Fort Collins was made in 1865 by D. Van Lennep. Though individual buildings are difficult to identify, the three-sided pattern is clear. The foothills to the west help orient the camp. *H00126*.

Jefferson Street, which becomes Riverside Drive, was once called the Denver Road and served as a thoroughfare of sorts when the town was settled after the fort closed. The other anchor for the main part of the fort was the Poudre River. In Special Order #8, Collins described it as

> *beginning in the center of the main channel of the Cache la Poudre River… thence south four miles, thence east four miles, thence north about four miles to the center of the main channel of the Cache la Poudre River, thence with the center of said river up to the main channel thereof following its meanderings to the place of beginning.*

The site was actually not square but more triangular, according to fort records as researched by Gray, due to the vagaries of the river's course, and it consisted of 6,168 acres. Mason's land composed the eastern boundary of the fort, closer to one mile than four.

Collins issued orders for the building of company and officers' quarters, a temporary hospital, corrals or stables and "other necessary buildings and conveniences." Barracks, officers' quarters and messes were built in a three-sided rectangle around the parade, the open ground where the troops gathered. The hospital, staffed by Dr. Timothy Smith, was some distance from the main quarters. The parade, a three-hundred-foot square of open land (typical of military forts at the time), was centered where Willow and Linden Streets intersect. There was also a guardhouse on the grounds, along

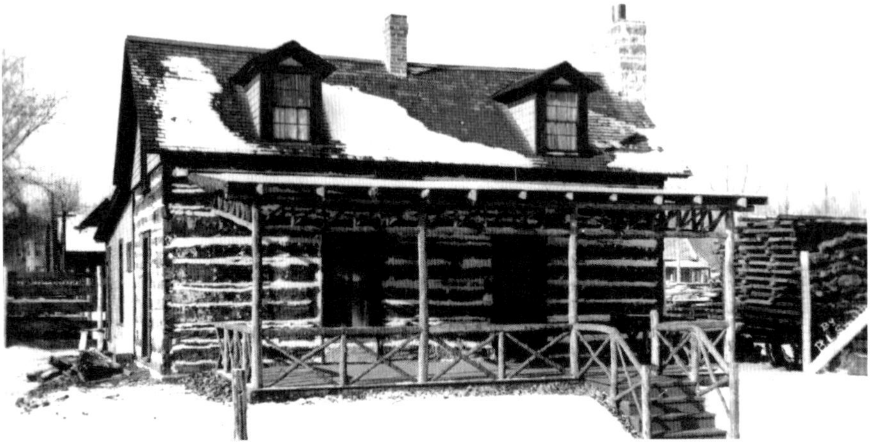

Auntie Stone's cabin served as an officers' mess, a boardinghouse and a hotel before being moved to the grounds of Library Park. *H00911.*

with a house for the laundress and privies. One pioneer, quoted in Evadene Swanson's *Fort Collins Yesterdays*, recalled that the horses were sheltered "under the bluff in dugouts" rather than in stables, but other sources assert that stables were built.

Made of logs, the structures would not meet our modern standards of comfort. Like its predecessor, Camp Collins, this fort was constructed by and for men accustomed to living in primitive conditions. The cabins were crude at best. They had hinged windows, as glass had to be imported and was very expensive; doors were vertical pieces of wood hung with leather hinges, not designed to keep out the cold. The same was true of the cabins inhabited by the civilians who came to the fort and settled in the immediate vicinity. Regrettably, no remnants of the original military post survive today.

Writing to his wife from the camp during the winter of 1865–66, Corporal Hiram Barney spoke of having to sleep alone on cold nights, his bunkmate having left the camp. The soldiers would spoon their bodies together at night to keep one another warm.

One of the first settlers in the fort, Elizabeth "Auntie" Stone came in 1865 with her husband, Lewis, to open an officers' mess for the troops. Their house was the only civilian dwelling allowed on the fort grounds. Unfortunately, Lewis died the next year, but Elizabeth and her family stayed on. Later, the house served as the town's first hotel. A two-story log house built by Henry

Peterson, the cabin was the scene of many jolly evenings, according to later accounts. Auntie Stone is reported to have danced the night away more than once, well into her eighties. In her book, Swanson reports that Auntie Stone's stepson, Lew, often called square dances at his stepmother's parties.

Years later, a former soldier named Patrick Glynn, who had been stationed at the fort and returned to New York, wrote a letter to John Coy, recounted in *A History of Larimer County*, in which he recalled buying milk from Mrs. Stone for $0.50 a quart and paying $1.50 for a pound of butter. He added, "'Who would want to live out there? No work going on; why one would have to live on prairie dogs and rattlesnakes.'" Another soldier, E.F. Ware, is quoted in the Watrous history as saying, "The country was bleak and arid and I would not have given ten cents a square mile for it. The whole country was desolate and forlorn, it seems to me."

Barney commented in letters to his wife that the cost of everything was high, and "the boys" entertained themselves at night by singing, reading and playing a card game of "bluff" (probably poker), during which many of them won or lost most of their monthly pay, other entertainments being in short supply. All of this makes one wonder why the first settlers who came—like Auntie Stone and her niece and Henry Peterson, who had been a gunsmith at the fort—stayed, along with a few others.

The first school in town began in Auntie Stone's modest house. Escorted by Peterson, Auntie Stone's widowed niece, Elizabeth Keays, came to Fort Collins in 1866 with her young son, Willie. Seeing that there was no school in the small settlement, Mrs. Keays began teaching her son and soon a few more pupils in one upstairs room of the Stone house. A school board was soon empowered, consisting of Captain Asaph Allen, W.D. Hayes and Peterson, and by the next fall, it had employed Mrs. Keays to teach in Fort Collins's first public school. Not long afterward, she resigned in order to marry Harris Stratton—married women being considered inappropriate candidates as schoolteachers at the time—but she had made her mark in history. Jesse Sherwood, who had become a county judge, married the couple in what is considered the first marriage between Anglos in the county. The public school moved to another building on the post.

Like others before and after her, young Mrs. Keays did not think much of the fort. Tribal uprisings had become more vigorous and deadly following the brutal Sand Creek Massacre in November 1864, but they had died down, at least around Fort Collins, two years later. The Civil War had ended with the Union preserved, and some soldiers had already been discharged when she arrived. She found the remaining soldiers lax in their duties and discipline minimal; she said she saw only one inspection, which the soldiers had to scramble to pass.

Yet the soldiers endured much. In January 1865, Lieutenant Hanna led about seventy soldiers of the Eleventh Ohio Cavalry from Fort Laramie to Fort Collins to reinforce Major William Evans's troops there. Protected only by buckskin, buffalo and beaver skins, the men rode along cheerfully, confident of arriving in good time, for the weather was bright and clear.

As they lay sleeping on the first night, it began to snow. When they woke in the morning, everything around them was dazzlingly white, and the temperature had dropped noticeably. They could not turn back; they had to keep going toward their destination. And they did—headlong into a full-blown winter blizzard. The snow swirled around them, blinding them; the horses bent their heads against the sharp, fiercely cold flakes. The wind cut through them like a knife. It kept getting colder.

They stayed close together, no one daring to fall behind. They well knew that coyotes and wolves awaited such tempting prey.

The empty, treeless plain offered no shelter. According to one soldier, who recounted the event years later as recorded in Watrous, no houses could be found between the two forts, nor was there a trail to follow. They were alone in a vast, empty, frigid wilderness.

At last they came to a likely spot and made camp, such as it was. Exhausted, disheartened and freezing, the horses lay down in the snow, seeming to understand their fate. Only their heads jutted up above the covering of snow. As for the men, they spooned as close together as they could, getting as warm as possible under blankets and snow. Regularly, the sergeant-at-arms would call out, "Spoon!" and as one they would roll to the other side without letting in the cold. It was, said the old soldier, "a night of horrors"—with more to come.

In the morning, they had to force themselves to keep going. Men were getting frostbite; horses were flagging and dropping down to feed the wolves. Some men appeared close to death, but their companions would not let them die, forcing them to walk or run until the deadly lethargy left them. Another day, another "hideous" night, the mercury about thirty below. Finally, the captain ordered the supply wagons dismantled for firewood. The men soon had a roaring fire to warm themselves and make some coffee. Alas, the fire did not last long; the wind blew it away, ashes, embers and all.

On the fourth day, having abandoned all their supplies and most of the horses, the soldiers experienced what, to them, was a miracle: the sun came out. It did not warm the air much, but the storm was over. They knew, then, that they would make it.

It was a ragged, frostbitten, bone-tired group of soldiers, men of iron will and boundless courage, who staggered at last into their new home—to recover from their ordeal and prepare to go out and do their duty all over again.

And the new arrivals did have skirmishes with Native Americans from time to time, to give the fort a reason for being there. During one of them, in July 1865, young Caspar Collins was killed. (Before he died, Caspar, who had enjoyed drawing as a child, made a sketch of the fort that survives today.) Assigned to Fort Laramie and inexperienced at soldiering, he had been leading a troop engaging with Cheyenne warriors at the Platte Bridge near present-day Casper, Wyoming. A wagon train had been surrounded, and Collins led troops to the rescue. When he saw a wounded fellow soldier caught amidst a group of braves, he dashed headlong into the mêlée to help. According to some accounts, his skittish horse, with a wounded man on its back, turned into the battle instead of away from it. Caspar didn't have a chance. In the end, five soldiers were killed, including twenty-year-old Collins, the only son of Colonel William O. Collins. Caspar is memorialized by the Wyoming town that bears his name (even though the spelling is different, probably due to a clerical error).

In their turn, the settlers had some disputes with the military troops. Several settlers had cattle, but with no readily available material for fencing, the herds roamed freely. Tempted to munch on the hay bales kept by the army for their mounts, the hungry animals were causing problems. Captain Evans posted guards by the hay so the cattle could not get to it and live to tell the tale. This development did not endear the settlers to the military or vice versa.

Watrous relates a story about an encounter with braves that happened in June 1865 near the fort. A band of Lakotas captured two wagons driven by soldiers and carrying supplies. The drivers escaped, reporting the incident to their commander, who promptly ordered pursuit of the warriors. In the ensuing chase, two soldiers were killed and possibly as many natives. One soldier who had been captured was later found dead, having been burned alive. The natives spared no quarter in protecting their hunting grounds. Augustine Mason, a brother of Joe Mason and also an early settler, described an altercation between the peaceable Arapahos and the more aggressive Cheyennes, who taunted Friday's people as cowards. Friday's son, Bill, took exception to that remark and shot the accusing Cheyenne dead. Young Bill was to pay for this impulsive act with his life, for even though he fled the area accompanied by his three wives, he was captured and killed when he later tried to return, his head set on a pole for all to see. His wives were taken captive by Pawnees, not to be seen again.

In 1866, General Tecumseh Sherman and General Ulysses S. Grant made a western tour and stopped at the fort. By then, the tribal attacks had slowed down (though not entirely stopped), and Sherman decided that the small fort was no longer needed. The general discovered that the troops were poorly equipped to fend off attacks, and he saw no reason for the army to sustain the fort. Accordingly, the encampment was abandoned in March 1867. While many of the soldiers stationed there returned home, some decided they liked the area and would stay around. Among them were Fred Wallace; George Buss, whose wife made and sold cheese; and Norman Meldrum, who had been a captain in the Union army and fought at Shenandoah and Williamsburg. Meldrum, a successful politician in the community where he chose to settle, served as a member of the territorial legislature and one term as lieutenant governor of Colorado and has a street here named for him.

Even with the decision of some soldiers to remain and most settlers to stay, there followed a period of about five years when the fate and future of the town hung in the balance. The abandoned fort was dismantled in short order, and settlers were scattered here and there around the valley. There was as yet no formal town. In nearby Wyoming, Cheyenne came into being in 1867 as a result of the westward expansion of the railroad—a technological advance that would ultimately spell doom for the Plains tribes.

In 1867, Jack Dow, Meldrum and others platted a town along the river, which flowed through the town at an angle. The next year, Joe Mason led a successful campaign to move the county seat from Laporte to Fort Collins. Old Grout, a remaining edifice from the fort, housed the county records and the jail. A few more settlers came. However, the land had not been released for permanent settlement by the federal government. The new town had yet to be born.

Chapter 3

In the Settlement

LIMBO

Who were some of the daring souls who remade their lives on the frontier? Auntie Stone was one of the first. Janis settled in Laporte, along with some other French trappers whose heyday had come and gone.

Some of those who settled here between the closing of the fort and the formal start of the town were soldiers who had remained. Others came to farm or to raise cattle or horses. Some, like Henry Peterson, came for the adventure of it and found a new way of life that worked for them. Some heard Horace Greeley's siren call, "Go west, young man!" and did just that.

Two of the earliest arrivals were John and Emily Coy, who were married before they left for the West and spent their honeymoon en route in 1862. California was their original destination; Coy had been there a few years earlier and hoped to go back. They left Cuba, Missouri, records Watrous, "with three yoke of oxen, a light covered wagon, a tent, a saddle horse and provisions." Although Mrs. Coy maintained years later that the journey had not been a hard one, at one point they were set upon by a robber who appropriated their small shotgun, and once their wagon got thoroughly mired in mud and had to be pulled out by passing soldiers. One night, most of their livestock disappeared; Coy spent several days searching for the animals without success. Delayed by the setbacks, the couple decided to winter in Colorado. They made their way to the Poudre Valley and just never got going again.

Descendants of the Coys tell family stories of the newlyweds taking up housekeeping in a small, somewhat damaged shack while John built a cabin.

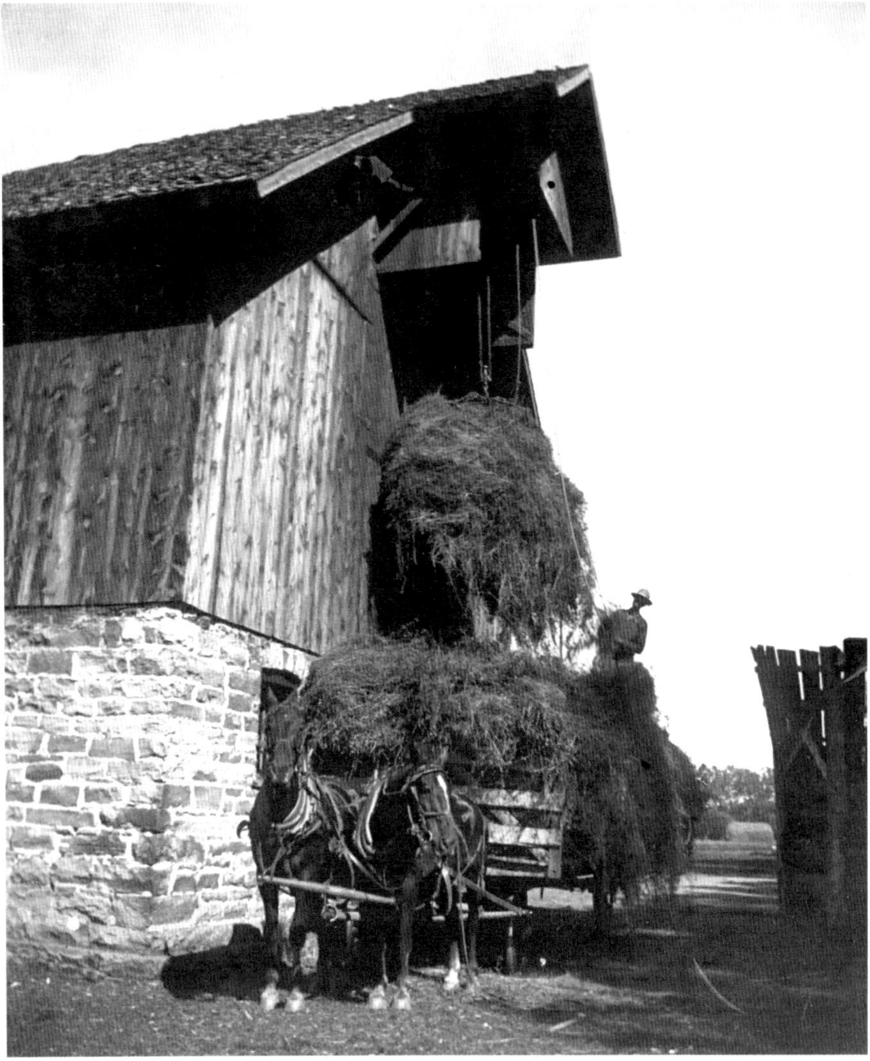

Built by John Coy in the 1870s, this barn is, remarkably, still standing, integrated into the new Woodward Company world headquarters on the site of what was once Coy's prosperous farmland. *H02443.*

Some of their children were born in the shack before the farmhouse was finished. The land they chose was along the banks of the river, east of the fort at the time, and was for decades a bountiful farm. Coy built his house on high ground to avoid the periodic floods. The Coy barn, facing onto Lincoln Street, still stands.

Young Lieutenant Hanna brought his wife to join him in 1867. At first they lived in a sod house with a mud floor, adjacent to a corral. Soon he moved her into another cabin with a sod roof and small, broken windows. She saw only a few cabins remaining from the fort—and a large tribe of Arapahos, who apparently did not intimidate her.

Yet the Native Americans had not given up easily. Faced with a tsunami of wagons rolling through their hunting grounds, they resisted in the only way they knew how, posing yet another hazard to those heading determinedly westward. It was not until the 1870s that the tribes capitulated in a war they at last conceded they could not win.

The emigrants did not give up easily, either. They continued to make their way west in a steady stream despite the many obstacles that faced them. Their migration was inevitable and unstoppable. The country was on the move.

Consider the pioneer woman. On the trail, she had to learn to cook over an open fire instead of on a stove (though many pioneers loaded stoves onto their wagons, they were very heavy, often abandoned and unusable on the trail in any case). She had to conduct her personal ablutions without privacy, endure day upon day of trudging forward with little more than optimism and faith to keep her going and sleep on open ground or, if enough possessions had been abandoned on the trail, in the wagon. Sounds, sights and smells of the prairie were probably new to her—the enormity of the darkness and of the night sky, the endless rolling prairie ahead, must have been a marvel. The profound silence, interrupted from time to time by the cries of coyotes, the hoots of owls, the sounds of small creatures rustling in the grass—all would have been a revelation to her, perhaps frightening, but she had to, as Eugene Smith said in his book about his mother, Sarah Milner Smith, "hide her fears and persevere."

And when the destination was reached at last, probably decided on by her husband or whoever was accompanying her, she had to learn even more: how to fire a weapon, for when her man was in the fields he was too far away to come to her rescue; how to wash clothes in an open bucket, swishing the fabric and suds around (for that matter, how to make soap); how to make do with whatever provisions were at hand; how to milk a cow; how to kill and gut a chicken or clean and prepare some other animal that had been hunted; and how to help out with the many chores farming and homesteading required. She had to haul water, build fires and keep them going and tend to the farm animals.

Undoubtedly, many of these undaunted women were already accustomed to doing such chores around the home—for women were largely confined to being homemakers then—but they would have had considerably greater resources at hand to do them, and the work would not have been so unrelenting, so essential for day to day survival and so lonely. With the homesteads spaced far apart, how they must have longed for the companionship of other women. Like Emily Coy, they probably would have had to give birth with little or no help and then care for the infant hoping for the best, clothing the babe in hand-sewn clothes (sewing machines were far too heavy to bring along, and they were cumbersome at best), nursing the child and dealing with whatever mishaps came along. Not all babies made it to maturity; in fact, in many families, more children succumbed to disease than survived. When that happened, the pioneer woman had the heartache of loss to cope with as well.

For there was no way to combat disease but to endure it and hope to survive, no way to deal with wounds but to bind them and watch and wait. They could trust only that the water they drank was pure enough, that the milk they squeezed from their cows was safe and that the meat they ate was not tainted.

It is perhaps no surprise that the western woman became tough, independent, capable and strong; that she resisted being restricted in her activities and thoughts; and that Wyoming became the first state to grant women the vote, followed by Colorado. For these women would not be denied and did not have, as their eastern sisters-in-spirit did, a history of cultural tradition and dominance to overcome.

Equally challenged on the trail, the pioneer man sat all day on a hard, backless bench, his arms straining at times to manage his team of oxen or horses. He was responsible for the safety of those traveling in his care—a wife and probably children. And what lay ahead of him? Endless prairie seldom relieved by trees or hills. On a good day, without impediments such as streams to ford, bogs to avoid or bad weather to contend with, he made twenty to twenty-five miles, with another stretch of prairie ahead. At night, he must have slept fitfully, half alert to sounds of danger, his rifle by his side. He had to take care of the animals, making sure they had grass to graze on and water to drink, and find food for his family; the provisions they could bring along must have been meager and would soon be gone. So he might have to stop from time to time to hunt prairie fowl or other game and perhaps to fish. His were the decisions to make—where the wagon headed, when it stopped, where they were to camp for the night. If he was in a wagon train, as many were, he would not have had to make these decisions alone, but the men had to accept the choices of the leader of the train even if they did not agree—that or leave the train and go on alone, not a desirable choice.

The hazards they faced were many and varied: hostile tribes seeking to hold back the tide of emigrants, lightning storms, hail or tornadoes, lack of water or game or firewood, injuries and accidents. James Michener, in his novel *Centennial*, describes sudden death from snakebite. Occasionally, a woman would give birth on the trail, sometimes with no one but her husband to tend to her.

Fire was an ever-present danger, as were rampaging herds of buffalo. And yet these men and their families pressed on.

Why did they come, so many emigrants? Volumes have been written about the westward migration. Many of the travelers kept diaries. From these documents and memories, it is possible to discern that most came for the promise of their own land. Some came because they had failed in some way at home and desired a fresh start. One memorable example of this situation is given to us by Jacob Flowers, who settled in Pleasant Valley north of town and named the new settlement Bellvue. Flowers had been a riverboat captain who lost two of his three vessels within half an hour and, having no insurance to recoup his loss, simply headed west to start over again.

Some no doubt just had itchy feet. Thousands were lured by the prospect of untold riches. And Lewis and Clark, along with other explorers, had described a wondrous land, full of natural beauty and abundant wildlife. Why should they not venture forth to see it? It was part of their own country, part of a country that they now knew stretched from sea to sea. What an adventure it would be to discover it for themselves!

A yearning for adventure was undoubtedly a factor when the Sherwood brothers came to the valley in 1860. Frederick and Jesse Sherwood came from Wisconsin. Hauling logs down from the mountains, they built a home along the river and raised horses, cattle, grains and vegetables. Fred Sherwood, who along with his brother was well known in the area by then, performed what is considered the first wedding in Larimer County on New Year's Day 1862. Approached by a young man identified by Watrous only as "Young Cyr," a son of Louis Cyr, Sherwood agreed to perform the ceremony in the absence of his brother, a probate judge. As they mounted their horses to go to the home of the bride, Cyr noted that Sherwood had no bible with him; when Sherwood told him a bible was not needed, Cyr insisted that he would not marry without one. Dismounting, Sherwood went into his house and brought out a large volume of Shakespeare's works, which appeased the prospective bridegroom.

As Watrous relates, the bride was found to be hiding under a blanket when they arrived at her home. Soon persuaded to show herself, she submitted to the ceremony, which lasted almost an hour and was witnessed by two visiting gamblers. As the couple prepared to depart, the father of the bride told Sherwood, "You make paper that if my gal behave and boy get drunk and raise the devil, my gal get all his horses. If my gal do wrong by Lewis he tell her go hell." The couple, Watrous records, appears to have lived happily ever after, as their names do not show up in any divorce records.

Considering an in-depth sampling of the early settlers, described by Watrous as hardy pioneers, some especially memorable ones are Henry Peterson, one of the very first to arrive here; Joe Mason, he of the fort relocation story; Timothy Smith, the fort's first doctor; William Stover, an enterprising businessman; Abner Loomis, an entrepreneur; and Agnes Mason, said to be the first Anglo child born in the valley. Each has a story to tell.

Peterson was searching for gold when he headed west in 1859. He came to the valley in 1864 and staked a claim, which he farmed alone. He grew hay and raised livestock, using feed sacks to make his pants because money was so scarce. With perseverance and grit, he prospered, becoming wealthy enough in a few years to help the widowed Auntie Stone build the town's first flour mill in 1867. The mill plan suffered a setback when Peterson went to Buffalo, New York, to purchase the equipment and was robbed in Chicago of about $3,000, a fortune at the time. He had to return to Fort Collins, raise more money to finance the new venture and then make another trip back east. This time, he was successful, and the mill was built. In 1870, the newly chartered Masonic Lodge met on the third floor. It was Peterson to whom Chief Friday recounted his tale of the battle between the Arapahos and the Pawnees. A Fort Collins street honors his memory.

According to the Watrous history, Joe Mason, a French-Canadian who anglicized his name from Messier, arrived at Laporte in 1860 after leaving a party of explorers searching for the headwaters of the Yellowstone River. He left Laporte again for a while but returned in 1862 and purchased land along the Poudre River. In October 1864, after the camp's move downstream in which he was so influential, Joe was named sutler to supply goods to the soldiers. Mason and a partner, Henry Chamberlin, built a store at the new fort, which was soon replaced by a sturdy building labeled Old Grout, so named because of the material with which it was built—a building, says Watrous, whose history "would read almost like a romance." It was a gathering place for both the soldiers and, after the fort closed, the increasing numbers of settlers. Mason sold a glass of beer for twenty-five cents. From the day he was appointed sutler until his accidental death in 1881, Watrous says, "amid all the trials and discouragements incident to pioneer life, he never lost faith in Fort Collins."

Trials and discouragements there were, to be sure. All in all, the years between 1867, when the fort closed, and 1873, when the new town began, were bleak. Although settlers trickled in, a drought took a severe toll on crops in the late 1860s and early 1870s. Coupled with that was an infestation of grasshoppers in 1872 and 1873, the likes of which had seldom been seen. The insects ate everything in sight, even clothes hanging on the line. Sometimes they were so thick that they blotted out the sun. Nothing was safe from their ravaging. Crops were decimated, trees and bushes stripped of their leaves, grass nibbled down to the soil. They descended in hordes, crunching hungrily, and then moved on. Soon, another horde would appear. Just walking around, people would step on hundreds of the insects. The noise of their whirring wings drowned out other sounds.

Farmers had no means of combating these dual assaults from nature. The concept of irrigation was in its infancy, and water was not abundant. No one had ever heard or even conceived of pesticides to rid the area of unwanted insects. It was said that turkeys liked grasshoppers, but farmers did not typically keep turkeys for domestic stock, and even those hungry birds could not possibly have consumed enough of the bugs to make any difference. Discouraged, many farmers gave up their homesteads and left. Watrous calls these "the dark years."

Just getting by posed many challenges: timber to build houses, for one. Trees to make fences and corrals resided high up in the hills and had to be harvested and brought down a few logs at a time, hauled by horses or floated on the river. Some essential supplies, like farm implements and seed, had to be imported from the East, perhaps as far away as Missouri. If farmers could not grow sufficient food to see them through the harsh, often bitter-cold winters, they and their families would go hungry.

Communication—dependent on the safe arrival of the mail—was only by a very slow, often unreliable mail service. Not infrequently, families who emigrated west were not heard from again by their eastern relatives. Journeys back and forth were fraught with hazards of weather; Native Americans fighting for their vanishing way of life; unchecked outlaws; and impediments like rivers to ford, prairie fires that swept through the plains with unstoppable ferocity and wagon trails that could easily turn into impassable mud.

Yet these early pioneers, who hung on with astonishing determination and courage, could see a better future. Industrialization had changed the nation—indeed, the world—and the railroad was marching westward.

Despite the soldiers' bleak assessments, the valley remained a fertile place with a good supply of clear water. More people were coming. Technology was advancing at a rapid pace. The world was changing.

Medicine, however, still awaited the period of discoveries about the human body and ways to treat its ailments that marked so much of the twentieth century. Dr. Timothy Smith, another early arrival who came to minister to soldiers at the fort, did not have many aids to help him treat the people who presented him with sicknesses and wounds. If surgery was required, the doctor could use morphine or laudanum, a more powerful substance, to render the patient unconscious. If he had none, alcohol was the next choice, though it didn't always dull the pain enough. Failing those two remedies, he had someone hold the patient down. No antibiotics or antiseptics were available—the patient was on his or her own to fight infection, which frequently followed surgery or digging out a bullet.

Dr. Smith also delivered babies. One of his most famous deliveries was of Agnes Mason, daughter of Joe Mason's brother, Augustine. Of course doctors made house calls in those days, and the good doctor was out on a call when Augustine came looking for him on October 31, 1867. Agnes was the Masons' first child; to find the doctor to deliver her, Augustine rode so desperately that his horse fell down and died. He had come to the valley because his wife suffered from respiratory problems, probably asthma, and after they got here, her health improved dramatically. Agnes, who was born in Auntie Stone's cabin, married Chester Giddings and lived out her long life in Fort Collins.

Like Joe Mason, Loomis came west in search of gold. He prospected with Janis for a short time. Arriving in 1860, he soon settled near Laporte. An enterprising young man, he harvested a large quantity of the abundant grass that grew in the valley, took it to Omaha, Nebraska, by wagon, traded for provisions, returned here and prospered as a rancher. By the early 1870s, he had been named a county commissioner. Until the building was demolished, commissioners' meetings were held in Old Grout, where county court was held, along with church services, theater performances and balls.

In the summer of 1868, records Watrous, a gang of horse thieves flourished in a camp near Owl Canyon, west of town. They stole horses and cattle; horses brought as much as $350, "no questions asked." The bold rogues, led by L.H. Musgrove, had even stolen a safe from the fort. Loomis finally caught Musgrove through a ruse, riding into his outlaw camp claiming to be unarmed and telling the gang leader about a loose horse he could easily catch. All Musgrove had to do was come with

Loomis, whom he had known casually for several years. They stopped for supper at Loomis's house and—surprise!—an armed Denver police officer entered the house and arrested the miscreant. Imprisoned in Denver, he was hanged by an angry mob that broke into the jail and hauled him out, erecting a scaffold on the Cherry Creek Bridge over the South Platte River.

With the departure of the soldiers, robbers became bolder during this fallow period. The stage line in particular was often victimized. But on one occasion, so the story goes, excess bravado played a significant role in a robbery. Stagecoach driver George Pritchett and guard Albert "Frenchy" LeBlanc knew they were running a risk when they set out on June 10, 1872, carrying a cargo of gold without a military escort. The driver and his guard weren't really concerned—both hardened mountain men, they were crack shots quite able and willing to shoot to kill. What was there to worry about?

Plenty, as it turned out.

Escorted by cavalry, the coach had arrived safely at the Namaqua stage station near Loveland, their precious cargo intact. But in the morning when they prepared to set out again, Colonel Oscar Critchell informed them that the army escort designated to complete the journey was away pursuing Utes. It could be a few days before the men returned; the stagecoach trip would just have to wait.

Nope, said Pritchett. They could make it without the soldiers. Reluctantly, Critchell agreed. Pritchett and LeBlanc set out toward Fort Laramie. They had not gone far, though, when the Borrell gang, father and sons, spotted the coach. No heads of passengers visible, no luggage on top—clearly, the coach was carrying something else, something valuable. Lurking behind boulders, the gang fatally shot the driver and his guard, calmed the panicked mules, grabbed the lockbox containing the gold coins and absconded into the hills to escape the soldiers they expected any minute.

Indeed, the cavalry was in hot pursuit. Regretting his decision, Critchell had dispatched troops to find the coach and escort it even though his men were not supposed to go that far north. The troops arrived just as the brothers were sprinting away. Ordered to stop, the gang kept running, getting far enough away to hide their booty—only afterward to encounter the Fourth Frontier unit returning from its pursuit of Utes. Confronted with weapons, the soldiers fired, killing all four gang members. One brother, Cobe, lived long enough to refuse, profanely, to tell the soldiers where the loot was hidden.

For weeks the soldiers searched the hills along what is now U.S. Highway 287—to no avail. Then civilians came by the hundreds, again with no success.

Years later, a civilian appeared to have found some gold, but he was unable to make a getaway before a gang attacked and killed him, and he, too, would not give up the location. The gold, if it exists, has never been found.

Clearly, vigorous law enforcement was a necessity. To this point, juries had been impounded on the spot and trials held promptly. This practice did not end with the establishment of the town, as later events illustrated, but Joe Mason was named sheriff in 1871. The enforcement of the law had become more formalized.

Another ambitious pioneer was William Stover, an early settler who came here in 1870 and opened a store in Old Grout in partnership with John Mathews. Stover served on the territorial council in 1873 and two years later represented the county at the constitutional convention that led to Colorado's statehood the next year. Stover bought a drugstore, which today is still in operation on North College Avenue as City Drug, the oldest continuing retail business in Fort Collins. The store prospered, and Stover became a prominent citizen in the new town.

For Fort Collins was indeed growing, despite setbacks of weather, insects, financial uncertainties, problems with lawbreakers and other tribulations. Undeterred by such obstacles, people were attracted to the beautiful valley, particularly to the county seat, where taxes were collected, judgments rendered and business transacted. The settlement of the estate of Captain Asaph Allen, a soldier who had stayed around after the fort closed, was the first significant case handled by the county court. Allen had headed east to buy goods for the general store, gotten off the train in Baltimore and disappeared "as though the earth had opened up and swallowed him," reports Watrous. No one ever heard from him again. No one knew of any relatives. His possessions had to undergo probate and be disbursed appropriately through the court.

Although Watrous states that from 1870 to 1872 "there was but little change either in the appearance or the business affairs of the town," some people did come, and more were on the way. The two-story National Hotel, built in 1870, provided respite for travelers.

But on May 5, 1872, Congress released the land held by the federal government for a military reservation. A new town was ready to happen.

Initiated by General Robert Cameron, the Larimer County Land Improvement Company organization consisted of John Mathews, William Pabor, Alfred Howes, Jared Bush, Reverend E. Hollister, Jesse Sherwood, Benjamin Eaton, John Remington, Norman Meldrum, E.W. Whitcomb, Jacob Welch, Benjamin Whedbee and Joseph Mason. This coalition represents most though not all of Fort Collins's early founders, several of whom have streets in town named for them. They called the new town the Agricultural Colony. The improvement company purchased three thousand acres connected to the original town.

Like many others who had made their way west after the war was over, Cameron was a veteran of the war who fought in several battles. Trained as a physician, he was a restless soul not content with settling down in Indiana, where he was practicing medicine. So when the war broke out, he rounded up a unit to join the Union army and quickly rose to the rank of major general. He incurred an injury to his eyes in one battle but did not lose his sight. Not only did he help with the Agricultural Colony here, but he also was instrumental in settling both Greeley and Colorado Springs. He did not remain in this area for long, however, going farther west to California and eventually returning to Colorado, where he died near Canon City in 1894. He is remembered here by Cameron Pass, which traverses the Continental Divide at the top of Poudre Canyon.

Cameron, along with the other founders of the colony, felt that the new settlement must have a moral foundation, attracting not ruffians and wanderers but families and individuals who would become solid citizens.

Accordingly, an 1872 brochure advertising the new colony informed anyone considering membership that those of "good moral character" could purchase one lot for $50, a business lot and a residence lot for $150 or the foregoing plus a water or railroad right

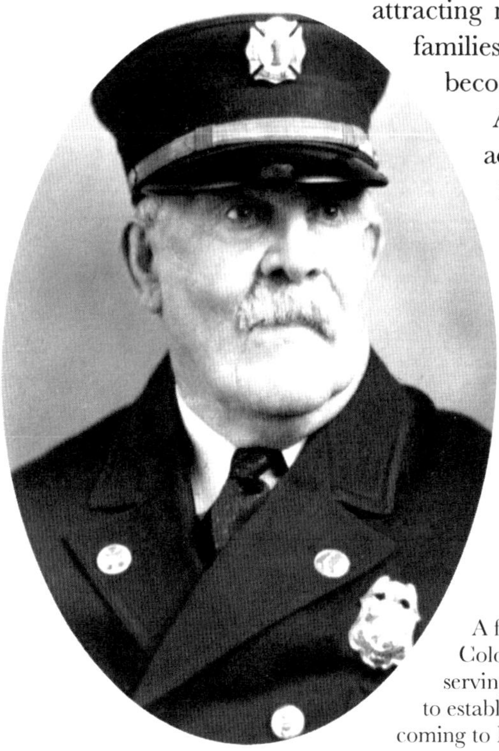

A founding member of the Agricultural Colony, Robert Cameron came west after serving honorably in the Civil War, helping to establish Union Colony in Greeley before coming to Fort Collins. *H08990.*

for $250. When the brochure was distributed, the *Denver Times* newspaper commented that the location was "one of the finest agricultural valleys in the territory." (Quite a different picture than that painted by soldiers stationed here.)

The brochure stated that the town had a general store; a drugstore; a brick mill (started by Auntie Stone and Henry Peterson in 1870); a schoolhouse on Riverside Drive, built in 1870; a post office; a flour mill; a blacksmith shop; and two hotels (both small, one being Auntie Stone's).

Enough potential settlers responded to the brochure that the dream of a settlement looked likely to become a reality.

The next year, Fort Collins taxpayers petitioned the county commissioners for incorporation. Twenty-three residents cast their votes. Duly elected as town trustees were Benjamin Whedbee, Henry Peterson, G.G. Blake, William Stover and W.S. Vescelius. The trustees elected Whedbee as president, Joseph E. Shipler as town clerk and Daniel O. Davis as constable. "The first important piece of business transacted by the board was to authorize the making of a road from the north end of College Avenue to the river, provided the County Commissioners built a bridge over the river at the intersection. Later the Commissioners appropriated $1,200 for the bridge and the road was built," notes Watrous.

A subsequent town election chose the same trustees and Shipler as town clerk, Albert Yale as street supervisor and E.L. Peterson as constable. The trustees appointed Ledru Rhodes (who built the first brick house in town, now demolished) as town attorney. These decisions and appointments thus established the rudiments of governance in the town.

It did not take long for the population to increase. Buildings went up quickly after the first drawing for lots on the first Tuesday in April 1873. Franklin Avery, who laid out the town, created blocks 400 feet square. Business lots were 25 by 90 feet, and residence lots were 50 and 100 feet by 190 feet. He made the streets wide—100 feet for residential streets, 140 feet for College Avenue (optimistically named)—commenting that there was plenty of room, and he intended to use it.

Avery, who did not name a street after himself, drew a lot just north of College and Mountain Avenues.

The wide streets, while providing plenty of room for wagons to come abreast of one another and to turn around, were an aggravation to the town's female residents, for they had to cross the dirt roadways, often covered here and there with horse dung, holding their long skirts up high enough to keep them from getting soiled. If the roads weren't muddy, they were dry, and dust rose up with every step. All pedestrians had to dodge

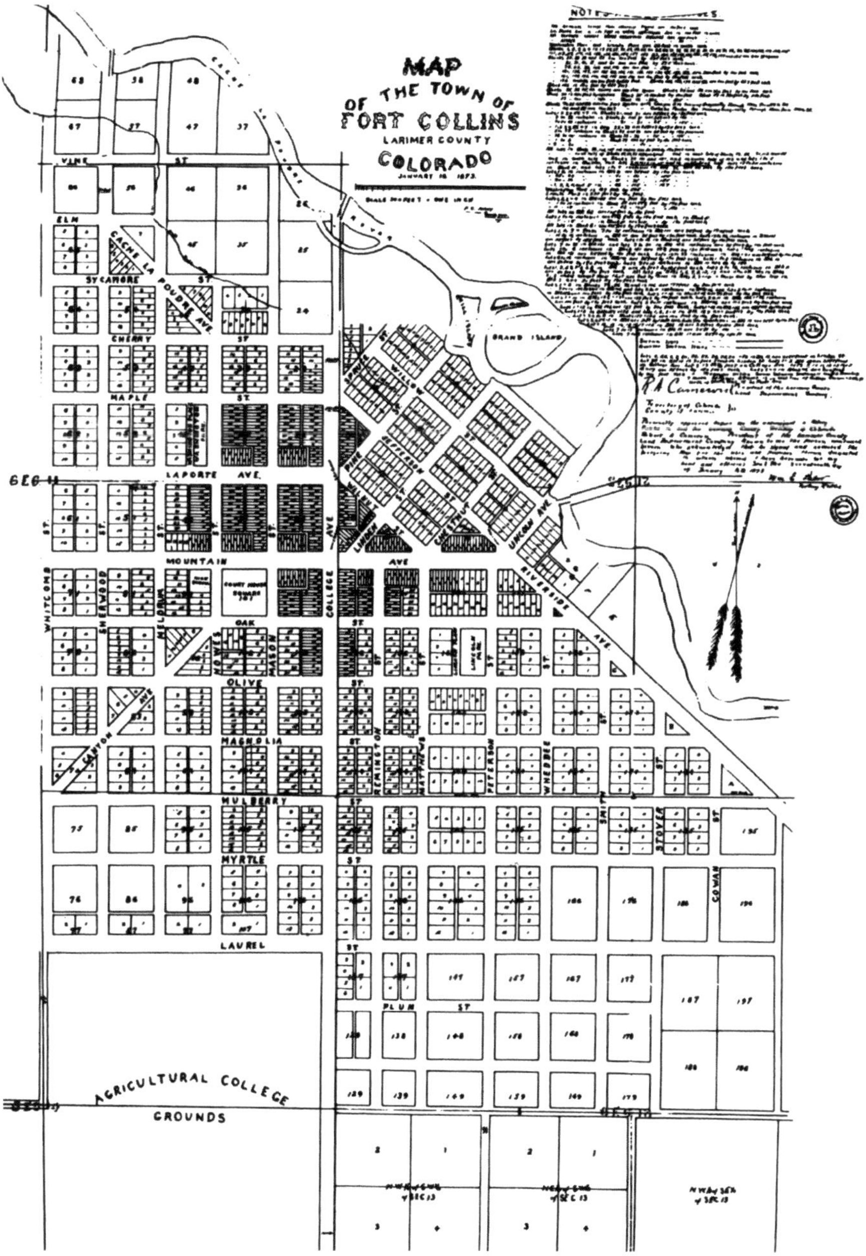

Franklin Avery laid out the new town, orienting it true north on 932 acres. Grounds for the college-to-be are clearly delineated in his plans. *FC00008.*

wagons and animals, but for the women, it was a particular trial just to make it across the street.

Avery, an engineer, oriented the new town true north whereas the original settlement had grown up angled along the river. The new town bumped into the old, creating a triangle between Jefferson Street and Mountain Avenue. Avery named the east–west streets after trees and shrubs and north–south streets after founders of the town. (Some of the names, according to Swanson, were chosen to conciliate residents already settled in the town.) Main roads were set a mile apart.

In fashioning a new town, the incoming residents paid scant attention to what had been there before, not considering that the fort they had replaced would be of any interest to future generations. Soon after the fort was abandoned, the structures in the fort were dismantled almost as if they had never existed, with the sole exceptions being Old Grout and Auntie Stone's cabin. This pattern of disregard for future generations' interest in the past was to repeat itself again four decades or so later, when historic structures along Jefferson Street were uprooted to make way for the new railroad tracks. It took until the 1970s for historic preservation to become important to the public and to municipalities.

Platting the new town on compass points put it at odds with the older town. When Whedbee relocated his store from Jefferson Street, in the older town, to College Avenue, in the new town, the move initiated a rivalry that continued for some time, the original town clinging to its roots and the newer portion striving for growth and progress. Some potential settlers were discouraged by the divisiveness, and newspapers, even political parties, took sides.

In spite of this conflict, growth went on apace. The little settlement was becoming a town. Rather than calling their new town Agricultural Colony, residents referred to it as Fort Collins, a name that recognized the fort that had been there not that long before. From camp to fort to town—a new era was beginning.

Chapter 4

Among the Pioneers

Settlement

The course of history for the new town was anything but smooth. Thanks to the grasshopper plague, crops failed. The town's first bank folded. The long-anticipated college had yet to materialize. More disheartened residents left. Others were lured away by tales of gold in the Black Hills in the Dakotas. By 1875, the population of the town was only about five hundred. Enough stayed to justify a few businesses, a newspaper, a livery stable, one church with a building and other congregations meeting in homes or other buildings and a bank.

The town, however, was not very appealing. The streets were rutted mud. Hitching posts in front of businesses meant that horses left their droppings behind. The odors can be imagined. Dust rose from the roads, flies were abundant, trees were sparse and the ground was sandy. Sanitation was lacking; water came from the river into which all manner of items had been cast, and outhouses were the order of the day. Law enforcement was minimal. Liquor was readily available. The male citizens didn't all go around with holstered guns as depicted in westerns, but there certainly were plenty of weapons around. Intrepid adventurer Isabella Bird, who came here in 1873, complained of locusts and flies and "coarse speech, coarse food, coarse everything…nothing on which the eye can rest with pleasure." She was decidedly unimpressed.

Women, being somewhat scarce, were treated courteously for the most part, although from the beginnings of the town, some houses of ill repute existed despite the founders' desire for a morally upright community. Children did have a school to attend. The civilizing influences of culture and religion were beginning to make a mark.

A promising start in that direction came when a lawyer, Jay Bouton (sometimes spelled Boughton), who had won a choice spot during the lottery for lots, raced to put up the first business on College Avenue. His law office, of the false-front variety much in use at the time, was the first of its kind in Fort Collins. By 1873, he had been appointed town attorney, and in 1876, he became the first elected county judge. Bouton had come to Fort Collins in 1872 to care for his brother, Clark, who was ill with asthma. Though Clark died two years later, Jay stayed on, married and became a prominent citizen of the town. In 1880, he introduced the kindergarten concept to Fort Collins, and the first one west of the Mississippi was held here that year. The idea spread; by the next decade, the state had made it a mandatory part of the school curriculum.

In general, it could be said that the decade of the 1870s was one of struggle and setbacks. The first buildings were frame, leaving them highly vulnerable to fire. The only sidewalks were made of boards, and there were few of those. There were saloons aplenty, a grocery, a drugstore, hotels, liveries and blacksmith shops and not much else.

Still, the pioneers held on to their vision of a prosperous town people would clamor to live in. And they did have reasons for hope.

By this time, the railroad was inexorably moving westward—clearly, changes were coming. All the communities along what has become known as the Front Range, the area in Colorado nestled east of the foothills from the northern to the southern border of the state, were eager to secure economic advantages. Boulder had acquired a university in 1861; Canon City was chosen for a penitentiary, and Denver won the competition with Golden for the site of the state capitol. Achieving the college for Fort Collins would, according to *Democracy's College in the Centennial State*, create a cultural center and attract an educated populace. Additionally, the research mandated by the Morrill Act would aid the struggling farmers. However, despite the selection of the college site by the territorial legislature, obstacles still stood in the way of its actuality. Aid from the federal government would have to wait until statehood, which was imminent but not yet achieved. What was needed was a site for the college and a claim—a building—to firmly establish the choice of their town.

A group of local citizens decided that the first step was to provide the land that would make the college possible. Greeley wanted the land grant college, too, so the push was on to ensure that the college came here. Several men donated land to that end: Arthur Patterson, Robert Dalzell, Joseph Mason, Henry Peterson and John Mathews. (Years later, Bill Cody, who had been a friend of Patterson's, came to town and wondered why no monument honored the donors. The college put one up.) In 1874, another early settler, R.Q. Tenney, who had been present with the Union army at Appomattox, had the honor of plowing the first row when the land was cultivated. Tenney had started a Grange chapter here; as grange master, he took the plow following a picnic the chapter had on the grounds.

The next step was to erect a building. The small brick structure, sixteen by twenty-four feet, was built the same year on the northwest corner of College Avenue and Laurel Street. A few years later, the claim building became the home of the college's first president, Elijah Edwards. With the college secured for the town (though not an actuality yet), the residents tackled another pressing issue. In the semi-arid high plains, rain was scarce, and the residents knew that in order to survive, the town needed a reliable source of water. By the mid-1870s, several ditches diverted water from the river, but they went to outlying farms. Drinking water for the townspeople came from the river or water wagons, which sold water drawn from the river at twenty-five cents a barrel, five cents a pail.

Not only was there continuing need for household water, but there was also the problem of fire. The wooden buildings erected during the excitement of establishing the town were all too prone to burn. The only way to fight fire then was with a bucket brigade, hauling water from the river or a ditch bucket

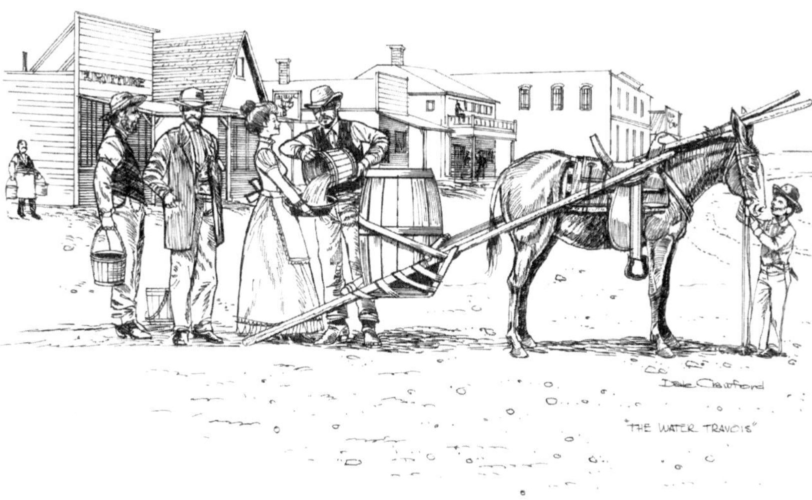

Ralph Coyte drew this sketch of the water wagon from which the townspeople bought water, which in turn came from the river. *Courtesy of Fort Collins Utilities.*

by bucket to be thrown on the fire. This method was slow, cumbersome and mostly ineffective, as well as being hazardous to those closest to the fire. A solution would not come until the next decade.

This time in Fort Collins was marked by a tragedy perpetrated on Native Americans who lived in the area. Having dispatched other tribes to reservations, the American government decreed in 1878 that the Oglala Lakotas must go live at the Pine Ridge reservation in South Dakota. Men living here who had married Lakota women were faced with a terrible choice: lose their land and leave their homesteads, their livelihood and their friends to go live with the Lakotas or divorce their wives, keep their land and stay in the area. Among many others, two men well known in the area, John Provost and Antoine Janis ("Yellow Hair All Messed Up," to the Arapaho) had Lakota wives and children by them. Janis chose to go with his wife and family to live out his life on the reservation. Provost stayed here. Either way, the choice had to have been an agonizing one for the men and for their wives—but it had to be made.

The 1870s were marked by growth in the cattle industry. Several ranches surrounding the town raised cattle; some raised sheep. E.W. Whitcomb, one of the first to bring in cattle from Texas, had a substantial cattle ranch north of town. (His was a memorable story—according to Swanson, he came west as a freighter and then, having lost his boots, walked one thousand miles through prickly cactus.) When the town was laid out, Whitcomb Street, which was named for him, was its western border. Other ranchers in the area were Abner Loomis, Joe Mason, William Stover and Benjamin Hottel. William Lindenemeier had vast holdings north of town. Most of the ranches were in the Livermore area. Despite the climate problems, the cattle and sheep ranchers prospered during this time, although there were occasional economic setbacks depending on the prices of beef and wool. A general panic in 1873 swept the nation. One casualty of this event was the failure of Fort Collins's first bank.

A.R. "Harry" Tutton opened the bank in 1873. He claimed that he kept the bulk of the deposits at a bank in Denver. When the national financial panic hit, he headed for Denver to retrieve the money, or so he claimed. He and the money were never seen again. Farmers who had counted on getting loans for seed were out of luck. Everyone who had deposited funds with the bank lost all of their money. It was a dark time. For some, barter became a necessity; some even bartered to pay their taxes.

Still, there was hope. Joseph McClelland came from Denver to start the county's first newspaper, the *Larimer Express*, in 1873. His first issue was four pages long and contained a promise that his newspaper would be on the side of truth, right and justice. Five years later, Ansel Watrous and Elmer Pelton started a second newspaper, the *Fort Collins Courier* (forerunner of today's local newspaper, the *Fort Collins Coloradoan*). Newspapers at that time were blatantly political—McClelland's was Republican and Watrous's Democratic.

A successful bank opened in 1873, owned by Mr. and Mrs. A.K. Yount. Charles Sheldon and William Stover opened another bank in 1878 that contained only a table, a couple of chairs and a borrowed safe. Louis Dauth, a German immigrant, came to town and opened a bakery in 1877 ("'fresh bread delivered to your door,'" quotes Swanson), and Joe Mason had a very busy livery stable. Other businesses were scattered along College and Mountain Avenues.

In September 1874, a telegraph line connected Fort Collins with Boulder, Denver and Cheyenne, enabling communication with "lightning" speed, according to the *Fort Collins Standard* newspaper (established in 1874 by Clark Bouton). Progress was happening in spite of setbacks.

Liquor was to be a matter of fiery controversy through the remainder of the nineteenth century. In 1873, an ordinance was passed to prohibit the licensing of establishments intending to sell liquor, but nearly seventy people petitioned for this ordinance to be repealed. When it was repealed in 1875, the cost of a license was steep. The first one, granted to T.J. Wilson, cost $150. This controversy would go on unabated until the mid-1890s.

Not only did McClelland start a newspaper, but he was also a highly successful fruit grower. His orchards along Fossil Creek were among the first in the area. With sufficient water from irrigation, the fruit he grew did well. The redheaded McClelland was known for his fierce temper. On one occasion, McClelland almost caused a cattle stampede when he fired a shotgun at a herd running through his orchard.

(A sight not at all unusual during this time was cattle being driven down the Denver Road, also known as Jefferson Street, on their way to market in Denver.)

Charles Pennock was another notable fruit grower. He experimented with various kinds of fruit, discovering what did and did not grow well in the valley climate. Knowing the longings of the settlers in the area for fresh rather than dried fruit, Pennock ordered many plantings of various kinds of fruit to discover what kinds would tolerate the altitude and climate. Many settlers had brought plantings with them only to discover that crops that had grown well where they came from did not prosper here. Pennock propagated the healthy varieties and eventually was successful enough to open the Pennock Nursery and Seed Company, which became known nationwide. Years later, he wrote an extensive, respected paper, part of which is reproduced in the Watrous book, on the results of his experiments.

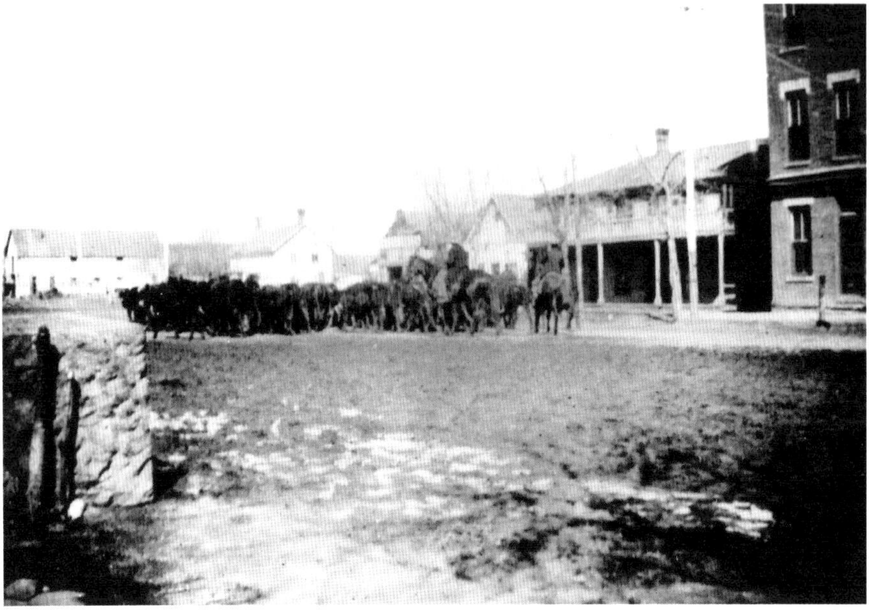

Cattle drives down Jefferson Street were not an uncommon sight in the 1880s. At right, the elegant Tedmon House hotel, dismantled in 1911, is visible. *H01985.*

Residents of our town celebrated with the rest of the state when Colorado was accorded statehood on August 1, 1876, thereafter being known as the Centennial State. This action allowed the development and governance of the state agricultural college, so it could finally be open for students: a state Board of Agriculture would oversee the new college.

The city management decided in 1877 that it was time to become official and incorporate in the state of Colorado. By a vote of forty to one in a special election in April, the ordinance passed.

Even though businesses were starting and newcomers were arriving and the college was underway at last, Fort Collins might have remained a small college backwater had it not been for the arrival of the railroad that same year. There were good reasons to lure the railroad. Getting produce or livestock to Denver for sale could take days and meant the farmer would be away from home for the entire journey. Settlers needed goods to equip their farms and build and furnish their homes. New residents could arrive more conveniently by train—as could tourists and students for the college.

Trains came through Denver and as far north as Longmont by 1870. A strong impetus for the arrival of the railroad was the poor, rutted wagon routes to agricultural markets in Denver, roads passable only when weather allowed. Farmers and ranchers needed their livestock and produce to reach the markets in a timely fashion if the town was to survive, let alone grow.

With W.A.H. Loveland lobbying hard for the Colorado Central Railroad to be routed through Fort Collins on its way to Cheyenne, city officials granted right of way approval in the spring of 1877. The town also provided land for depots and railroad yards. Grading for the tracks began as soon as the weather permitted. The tracks, laid north to south along Mason Street, were right in the center of town (a choice later generations came to regret).

The telegraph was an essential element to train routing and, consequently, safety. Loveland's nephew Thomas Montgomery arrived in town to be the first station agent and railroad telegraph operator, opening his office in Joe Mason's store on Jefferson Street until the new depot was completed. A smaller depot deposited passengers right on the campus.

On October 8, 1877, the residents of Fort Collins heard the first long, low whistle of an oncoming train. It's said that the smoke from the steam engine could be seen for miles as the train puffed its way toward town. The closer the train got, the more excited onlookers became. The train arrived in Fort Collins to the ecstatic cheers of residents assembled on either side of the tracks. A few days later, the first freight shipment arrived in Fort Collins, containing merchandise for William Stover's store and coal for Billy Patterson.

With the arrival of the railroad came hotels, for passengers would surely come to Fort Collins on the train and need a place to stay. One of the first hotels besides Auntie Stone's was the Commercial, which later was relocated to the corner of Walnut Street and College Avenue, setting the stage for what would become the Northern Hotel.

Hotel developers were right; people did arrive on the train, and hotels competed to be first at the station with a coach and four to take them directly to their establishments.

Ironically, the founder of one of the first banks in the town, A.K. Yount, was run over by a train elsewhere in 1876. With the fortitude and determination so evident in pioneer women, Ella Yount continued to run the bank until 1883, becoming a prominent citizen of the community.

So began, says Watrous, a new era in Fort Collins, bringing the town "in touch with the rest of creation," benefiting consumers, producers and merchants alike. As the visionaries had hoped, the railroad's arrival also brought settlers, able to bring with them their household goods and even farm animals and, as the college officials had hoped, new students as well.

The new college was finally up and running by 1879. A state funding act had levied an assessment on taxable property to finance construction of buildings at the new school, and a state Board of Agriculture was created to govern the institution. Tax collections yielded $8,000 to erect the first building, thereafter known as the Main Building, later called Old Main. A three-story brick structure with classrooms and a theater/auditorium, it was completed in 1879 with a façade of brick from Auntie Stone's kiln. On the first day of September 1879, the new president, Elijah Edwards, and his two faculty members, Ainsworth Blount and Frank Annis, welcomed five students (two of whom were relatives of the president) including one woman. By the end of the first term, there were twenty students to study arithmetic, English, history, philosophy, horticulture and farm economy—one course of study for all. Students were required to work at various manual jobs, for five or ten cents an hour, and to attend chapel services every morning. With the lack of preparatory high schools in the state—high school being a concept not widely in practice at the time—students as young as sixteen were learning then what future students would later learn in high school, according to Hansen.

The students studied algebra, geography and rhetoric in the winter; algebra, bookkeeping, botany and rhetoric in the spring; and in the summer, geometry,

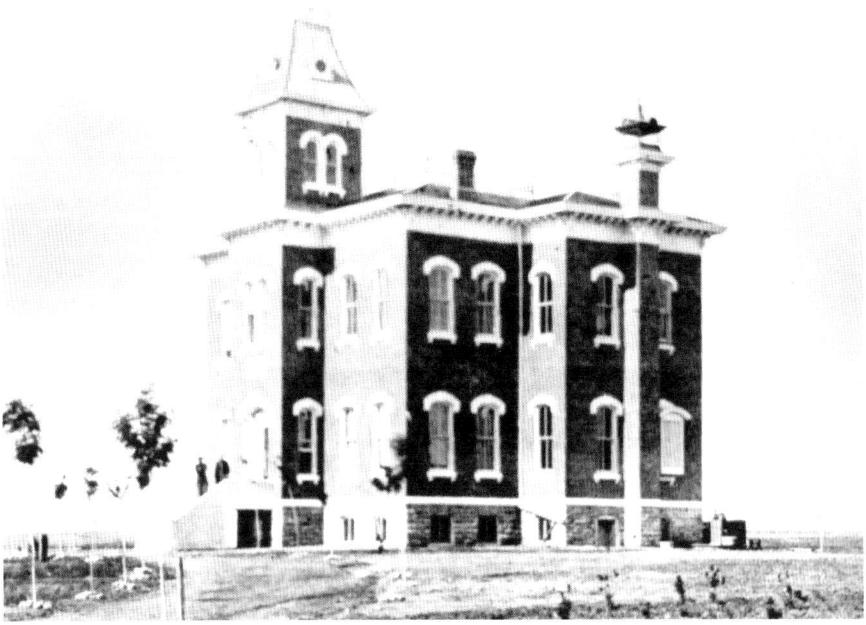

Perhaps the best-known and surely the most beloved building on campus, Old Main stood for nearly one hundred years. It was torched in May 1970 during a period of student unrest; the arsonists were never caught. *H00137.*

botany and history. Sometimes the lack of academic preparation on the students' part resulted in what today would be called remedial classes, particularly in grammar and arithmetic. Unlike many colleges of the time, this one was coeducational from the outset, and provision was made in the curriculum for women's studies by offering literature, history, art and science. The cultural expectation of the era was that women would marry rather than pursue a career—certainly not do both!—and indeed, some of the women who initially enrolled did leave college to marry.

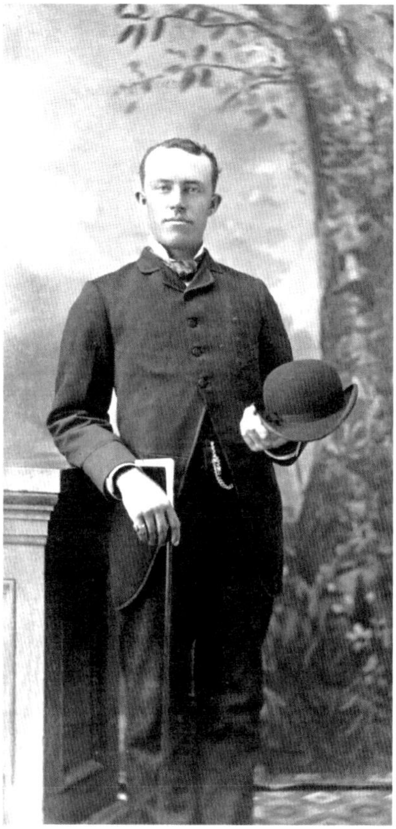

Coming to the college as a shy young man, George Glover earned a degree in veterinary medicine and paved the way for the university's highly regarded veterinary medicine school. *H14563.*

Old Main not only contained the first classrooms but also housed out-of-town students (many students lived nearby and walked to the school), some professors and, for a time, the college president and his family. The institution had challenges. With the trains rattling by at times during the day, all activity came to a halt because of the noise. That situation continued throughout the nearly one hundred years that Old Main stood. When the trains went by, classes would pause; actors would freeze in place.

One notable early student at the college was George Glover, who had come to Fort Collins from his family farm. The family had moved to the Longmont area because of Glover's mother's ill health. Though needed on the farm, Glover was urged by his mother to continue his education. So he set out with a horse-drawn wagon containing bedding, clothes and food to take up college studies and work as a janitor to help pay for his education. Arriving after what Hansen calls a "long, cold journey," he settled into a basement room, shy and uncertain about this bold move. Glover did complete his academic studies and would go on

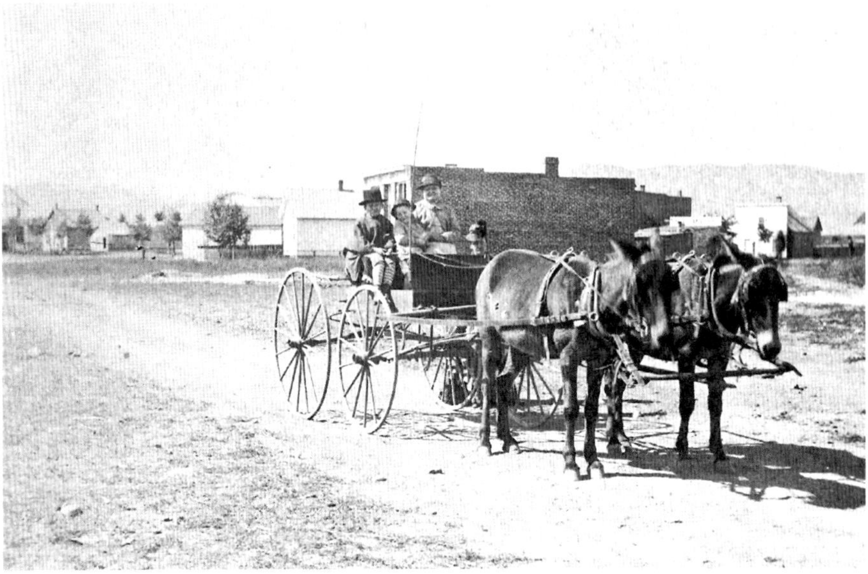

Sometime during his stay in Fort Collins, photographer James Shipler took this photograph, titled "A View of Fort Collins 1877," of a family preparing to enjoy an outing. *Courtesy of Malcolm McNeill.*

to become dean of the School of Veterinary Medicine, which he would help establish.

Then and for many years to follow, the study of veterinary medicine was focused on large domestic animals—horses, cattle and sheep. It would be the middle of the twentieth century before the emphasis shifted toward dogs and cats. Just as the horse was crucial to the daily life of the soldier of a decade earlier, so was it critical to the residents of any western town. Although it was illegal for a horse to come up on the sidewalk, this animal was so essential to daily life that citizens placed a horse trough right in the middle of town—at College and Mountain Avenues—so the horses would never be thirsty when they came to town. (The fountain was moved when streetcar tracks were laid.) Cattle and sheep provided a rancher's livelihood; his horse got him from here to there and back again.

With the trains coming to town, bearing passengers and merchandise, and the college a reality at last, the future for the town looked brighter. The college provided a sound economic base, and the trains connected Fort Collins with other communities. The small military outpost, once so isolated, was maturing into a community with justifiable hopes for a prosperous future.

Chapter 5

Beyond the Beginning

PROSPERITY

Although the nation was in an economic downturn, Fort Collins was well established as a successful community by 1880. The town contained the county seat, a college with ever-growing enrollment and faculty and a train station for passengers and freight, along with being surrounded by farms and ranches growing produce and grains and raising livestock, both cattle and sheep. Still very much dependent on agriculture for survival, the community nonetheless was progressing in other ways with new businesses and new schools. Then, in 1880, along came the telephone.

This new invention, so astonishing to many, was creeping westward. Frank Stover had a device installed in his home, connected to his drugstore. Newspapers of the day confidently anticipated that soon every household would have one.

In 1880, the city, now large enough to be declared a second-class city (population from 1,500 to 15,000), changed to a mayor-aldermen form of city government. Four wards were created. Mayors had one-year terms. Fort Collins's first mayor was David Patton, who favored high license fees for establishments selling liquor. The town proudly welcomed a new city hall, sharing space with the fire department, on Walnut Street in 1882. (The building, still standing, bell tower and all, is now a private business.) When the telephone came to town, a connection was soon set up between the fire department and the waterworks.

Yet despite all this progress and all the civilizing influences, Fort Collins remained a frontier town in many ways, with an abundance of saloons and brothels, as well as gambling establishments. Drifters and idlers were drawn to these attractions and created numerous problems. The first murder recorded in town happened on Christmas Eve 1881, when William "Tex" Lindeville shot and killed Albert Sherwood, an African American man who worked as a cook at the Tedmon House hotel. The shooting occurred at one of the bawdy houses in town, apparently after a brawl. The shooter was acquitted, pleading self-defense.

Tedmon House, described in local newspapers as one of the finest hotels in Northern Colorado, was built in 1880 by Bolivar Tedmon. A striking brick structure on Jefferson Street, three stories high with sixty-five rooms, it was considered very modern, featuring a dining room, barbershop and wall-to-wall carpeting. At the depot, a carriage awaited passengers to transport them to the hotel.

Just across the street on the south side stood Collins House, one of the first hotels built in town and the first to be built with Auntie Stone's bricks. On College Avenue, Jacob Welch built the Welch Block (a block being a building rather than the distance from intersection to intersection) in 1880; it housed the elegant Windsor Hotel on the second and third floors.

Commerce was healthy: the town had hotels, banks, liveries, general stores, drugstores, grocery stores and other businesses to counter the less desirable establishments. There were several banks, including the Poudre Valley Bank, designed by Montezuma Fuller and built on the northwest corner of Walnut and Linden Streets in 1882, which had a pole in the middle of the doorway in order, it was said, to prevent robbers on horseback from riding in. William Stover and Charles Sheldon operated this bank in competition with the First National Bank in the Welch Block.

Fuller had come to the area in 1880, twenty-two years old, trained and skilled as a ship's carpenter but not as an architect. In fact, he had no formal training in architecture but was asked to design a building for the college, where he was a special student, launching his noteworthy career here. Among other buildings he designed (including a house for a woman who was to become his wife) was the Avery Block at the northeast corner of College and Mountain Avenues, built in 1897 as a bank and today occupied by local businesses. As the town's first architect, Fuller went on to develop a thriving business in Fort Collins, earning a stellar reputation that has endured to this day. A downtown alley bears his name.

Brisk commerce was one aspect of community life, but residents still faced problems: a source for water, the proliferation of saloons and the ever-present danger of fire.

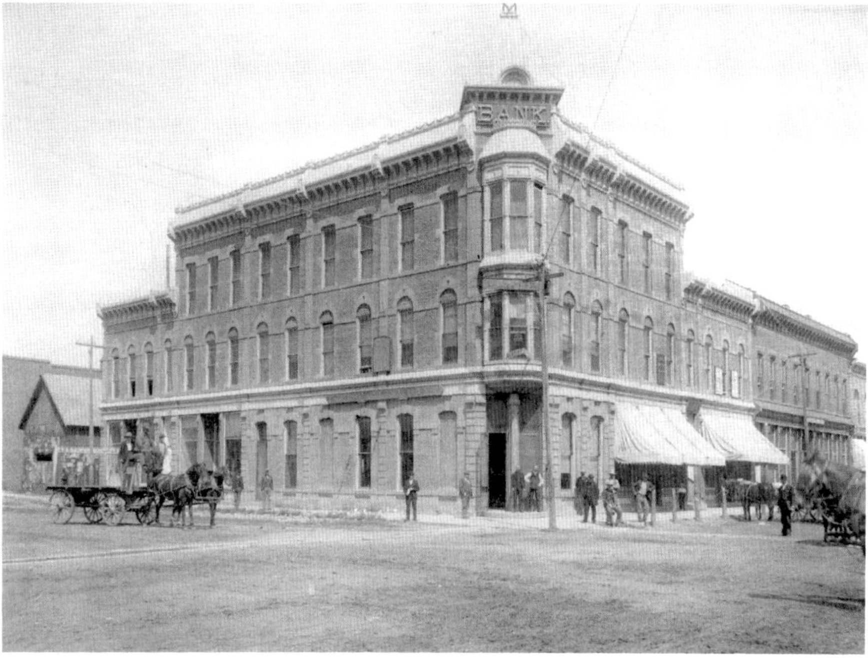

Note the pole in the middle of the doorway of what was then Poudre Valley Bank, put there to deter a robber attempting to enter on horseback and then make a quick getaway. *H05123.*

In 1883, Chloe Foster's house of ill repute burned down while people simply stood by and watched. Watrous comments that saloons would offer firefighters free drinks after a fire, which might have been a motivation for arson—although in this case, a woman "boarding" at the house blamed the fire and the lack of will to fight it on moralists. Could it have been deliberate? Nothing was ever proven.

All the saloons and consequent problems resulted in the formation of a local chapter of the Woman's Christian Temperance Union (WCTU) in 1880. The women began a vigorous crusade to rid the town of demon rum. Despite the setback of the liquor ordinance being set aside, the women continued their campaign.

Safe water to drink was another major issue. Up to this time, water had been drawn from the river. Many residents bought this river-drawn water from a water wagon, but it was the same water—unsanitized and impure. Plus, when there was a fire, the only recourse was the bucket brigade, ineffective at best. In 1880, the Welch Block caught fire, killing two young people who had been trapped inside and destroying the Windsor Hotel,

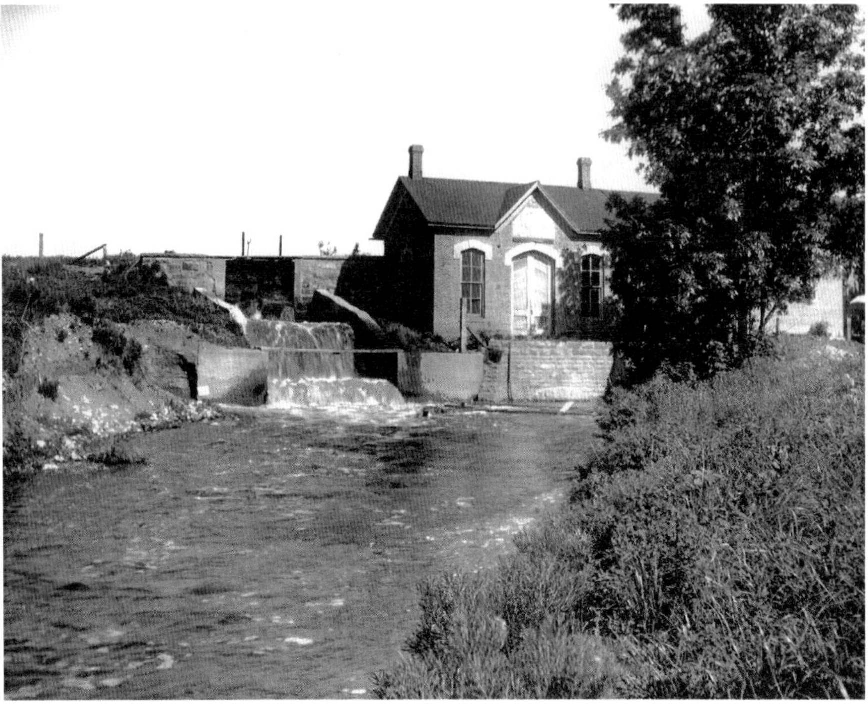

Built in 1882, the Overland Trail water delivery plant collected water from the river and sent it to town via gravity feed, enabling more efficient firefighting. It is currently undergoing restoration. *H19369.*

which was not rebuilt. It was clear to the residents that a better firefighting method was essential.

Convincing residents of the necessity for a waterworks to supply a reliable stream of water for fighting fires was easier after the Welch Block tragedy. Accordingly, the Fort Collins Waterworks was constructed in 1882–83 north of town on Overland Trail. Building the waterworks led to the formation of a team of volunteer firefighters, ready at a moment's notice to be at the scene and hook up the hoses. Twenty fire hydrants were installed. The fire department recruited young men who could run fast. The more quickly the wagon and hoses could get to the fire, the less likely it was to spread. This fostered competition among hose teams in nearby towns; one year, when Fort Collins won, the team was accused of recruiting a ringer.

Praising the new waterworks, Watrous notes, "Fort Collins then had, in the opinion of experts, as good a system of water works as there was in the state and naturally the people were proud of it. They also appreciated more than words could express the privilege of turning a faucet in their own kitchen and getting an abundant supply of pure water for all uses."

Not really so pure. The water was not filtered (except for "logs and dead horses," it was said). It was not really safe to drink, as would be discovered in due time.

Meanwhile, progress continued slowly but surely. By this time, the school district found itself having to rent space for classrooms, and it was determined that a new school was direly needed. Remington School, built in 1879, was full to overflowing. At a cost of $19,500, Franklin School rose on the southwest corner of Mountain Avenue and Howes Street in 1887 to accommodate all the new students. Proposed by Edward Lyle, a high school program began at the school in 1889, eliminating the preparatory classes that had until then been necessary at the agricultural college. High school classes were held on the second floor of Franklin School until a new building went up on the southwest corner of Howes and Magnolia Streets in 1903.

The college, too, was experiencing change and progress. More departments were created, more professors were hired and the student body grew. With its mission to improve agricultural practices, the college

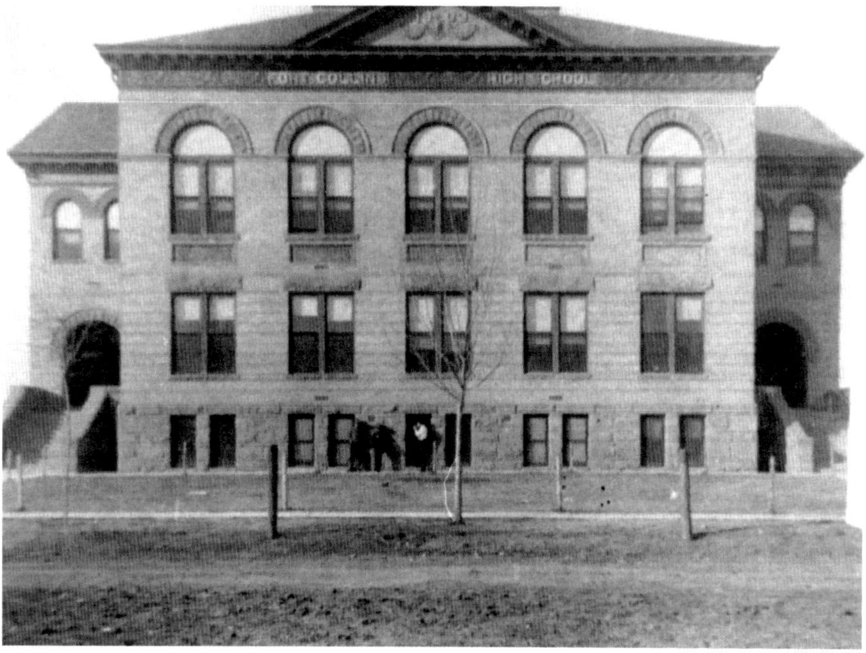

The first high school in Fort Collins, where the Lincoln Center is now, became Lincoln Junior High School in 1925. It was built in 1903 at a cost of $50,000. *H00811.*

became involved in developing irrigation methods. Especially prominent in this work was Elwood Mead, who went on to achieve national acclaim and have a body of water—Lake Mead in Nevada—named for him. The college also became more invested in the care of livestock, since so many people depended on horses for transportation and cattle for livelihood. Hansen reports that George Glover got the job of inspecting Texas cattle for a deadly fever with the force of law on his side. Since the college land was still a working farm, livestock were quartered and cared for there and had to be protected from disease. By 1883, veterinary science had become a course of study at the college.

Development of the Farm Institute at the college foreshadowed the creation of the Agricultural Extension Service. In 1888, the college began the experiment station still operating today, which was a great help to the farmers in need of ways to deal with insect infestations, drought and water delivery. The experiment station was to play a significant role in the development of the sugar beet industry here.

In 1883, the college began a dairy herd that would endure for almost one hundred years. The arrival of a jersey cow and her calf was the beginning of the herd, first housed slightly south of the campus. The domestic sciences curriculum for women included the making of butter, and the studies in dairy science aided farmers.

Women were offered alternatives to agricultural studies, but the fifty young women enrolled, declared Professor Charles Ingersoll, deserved at least one female faculty member. With the hiring of Elizabeth Bell in 1886, the college expanded its liberal arts offering and diversified the faculty. When Miss Bell developed ill health, her sister, Maud, was hired in her stead. Other female faculty members were soon to follow.

One visible sign of prosperity was the construction of several large, well-appointed new homes. Architect Fuller's own home on West Magnolia Street was a Victorian gem, and Franklin Avery, who had become a prominent businessman in town, built a large home on West Mountain Avenue in 1889. He lived with his wife, Sara, and their three children in the home that is now listed on the National Register of Historic Places. The house, with its distinctive sandstone façade, was symbolic of the prosperity the town was beginning to experience. By this time, nearly all of the town platted in 1873 had been filled in with houses, churches and commercial buildings. Though the downturn churches are mostly gone, as are some of the commercial buildings, many of the homes built during this era remain today. The town was starting to expand beyond its original boundaries.

Another house with a distinguished history is the James Arthur house, at 322 East Mulberry Street. Coming to Colorado in 1859 to search for gold, Arthur soon discovered the high value of hay, in those days much more lucrative than the precious metal. Living in a tent, he harvested and baled hay. At that time, hay was baled with a box. Pitched in, tramped down and wrapped with rope, it was then ready for transport and sale. There was only one problem: Arthur found the boxes of hay too bulky to manage alone. So he and a partner, John Hahn, acquired an old cotton press and used it instead. According to a 1963 article in the *Coloradoan* newspaper, this was the first use of a cotton press for such a purpose west of the Mississippi.

Arthur left a lasting legacy when he created a private ditch company in 1862 to divert water from the river for irrigation and domestic use. Subsequently, other ditches were dug through the town in later years; the Arthur Ditch still exists.

Prospering with his hay business, Arthur soon turned to livestock, driving a herd of cattle from Missouri to his farm. By then well-to-do, he built the distinctive Victorian home and later became a county commissioner, state senator, bank president, city council member and mayor. When he died in 1905, the *Fort Collins Courier* described him as "the most charming of men, genial, kind and obliging."

Cultural offerings were expanding along with residential growth. Piqued at being known as a rough frontier town, a "cow town," some local citizens decided to introduce culture into the community. A consortium of local businessmen decided to build an opera house, a popular venue since the advent of miner Horace Tabor's opera house in Central City, Colorado. Following the fire that destroyed the Welch Block, Welch joined the other investors to build the Opera House Block. The opera house featured pillars, arches, murals and contemporary art and attracted audiences for minstrel shows, dramas, tableaux, nationally known speakers and other offerings in vogue at the time. One of the most popular offerings was the play *Uncle Tom's Cabin.*

To further enhance the cultural scene, Lincoln Park on Mathews Street, set aside along with Washington Park when the town was platted in 1873, acquired a bandstand and more land so that it took up the entire square block. Culture and recreation were growing in importance. In 1884, sign painter and artist Pierre Dastarac drew a map of the town that showed some of the prominent structures and depicted Fort Collins as a civilized, settled community.

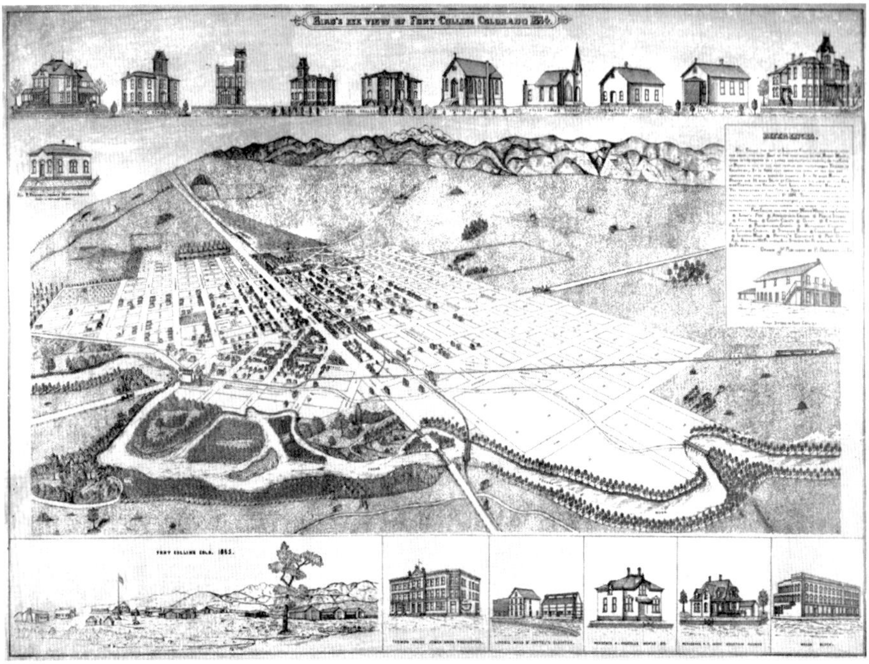

Pierre Dastarac, who worked as a sign painter, created this bird's-eye view of Fort Collins in 1884. When he moved to Denver in 1896, he left us this depiction of our town during a peaceful, prosperous time. *H00044.*

Commercial enterprises were also doing well. When Joe Mason died in 1881 after being kicked by a horse, Benjamin Hottel purchased the gristmill that Mason had owned. Swanson notes that a major hazard of milling was fire due to the dust that accumulated. Such a disaster—an explosion—happened in July 1886. Fortunately, the fire brigade was on hand. The mill was rebuilt and operational later that year. (The mill, now Ranchway Feeds, is today the longest-operating industry in Fort Collins.)

Swanson also records the growth of the horse-breeding industry in the area. Horses were needed for work and transportation, of course, but there was also high interest in horse racing. Jesse Harris had a highly regarded livery stable on Jefferson Street. Several local men were very skilled in handling horses, using Old West techniques. Harris imported horses from England and began breeding. Some of his stock sold for more than three figures, quite high value at the time.

Regrettably, horse racing enticed gamblers. In one notorious incident at Tom Earnest's track southeast of town, Earnest learned that out-of-town

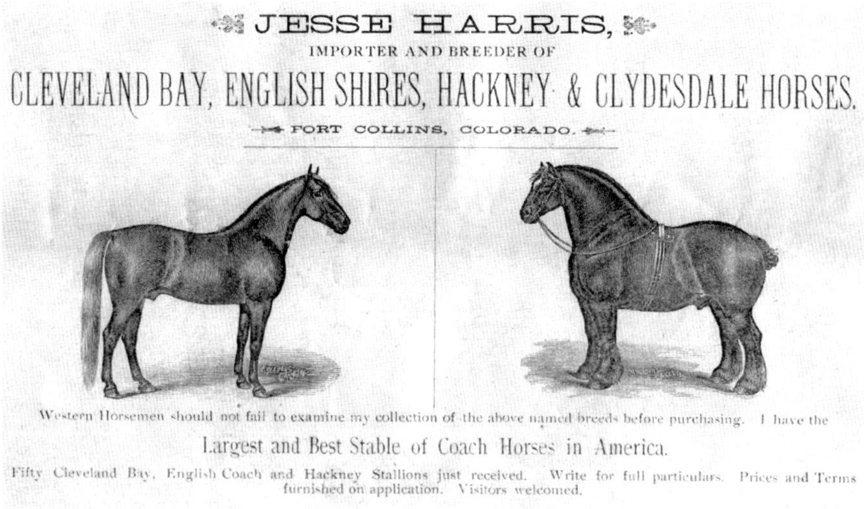

An advertisement for the Harris Stable illustrates the importance of horse racing. Jesse Harris was well known in the area for the quality of his stock. *H19428.*

gamblers planned to fix a race at his track. When the race began, onlookers were startled to see Earnest on horseback beside his entry in the race, one hand holding the reins and the other a revolver. If Earnest's jockey should lose, Earnest's firearm implied, the jockey was a dead man. With such compelling motivation, the jockey won, although Earnest almost beat him to the finish line.

Counterbalancing the seamier side of life here, churches were beginning to appear. Presbyterians had organized in 1872 and met in a building at Walnut and Linden Streets; a decade later, St. Luke's Episcopal Church, a small stone structure, graced College Avenue. Catholics had a presence here in a wooden church on Mountain Avenue at Riverside Drive. Methodists had a building at Mountain Avenue and Walnut Street. The First Baptist Church on the northeast corner of Remington and Magnolia Streets was constructed in 1881, and the Presbyterians built a small church on the southwest corner of Remington and Olive Streets in 1877.

For those who sought it, ample work could be found. A quarry opened at Stout, producing sturdy sandstone blocks. It did not take long for the wooden sidewalks in town to be replaced with stones from the nearby quarry. Railroad lines were laid to transport the stone. The quarry was the largest employer in the area, with stone being used to construct buildings and train stations. The town of Stout was also the scene of considerable mischief and mayhem, offering diversions that were gradually being edged out of Fort Collins as more families settled here.

The railroad brought stone from the quarry to other cities, including Denver. The Greeley, Salt Lake and Pacific Line (GSL&P), affiliated with Union Pacific, which served the quarry, was incorporated in 1881 and had every intention of creating a transcontinental line through the heretofore resistant Poudre Canyon. By that time wagon trails wound up the canyon. In 1881, according to author Norman Fry, the wagon roads were widened by heavy traffic after silver deposits were found in the mountains, and two mining towns, Teller City and Lulu City (both ghost towns now), sprang up.

Manhattan, another mining town north of the canyon, played a part in the story of one of our town's most memorable characters, Lady Catherine Moon. An orphan from Ireland, she began life here as a laundress at a mining camp in 1883, married a miner and then divorced him to marry an Englishman, Lord Cecil Moon, whom she had nursed through an illness. Their time together was tumultuous, but they did travel to England when Lord Moon inherited the baronetcy. The highlight for her was meeting Queen Victoria. With the inheritance, they bought a ranch, which was much more suited to her than to him. Eventually they divorced, but she retained her title and paid her ex-husband alimony with income from the ranch.

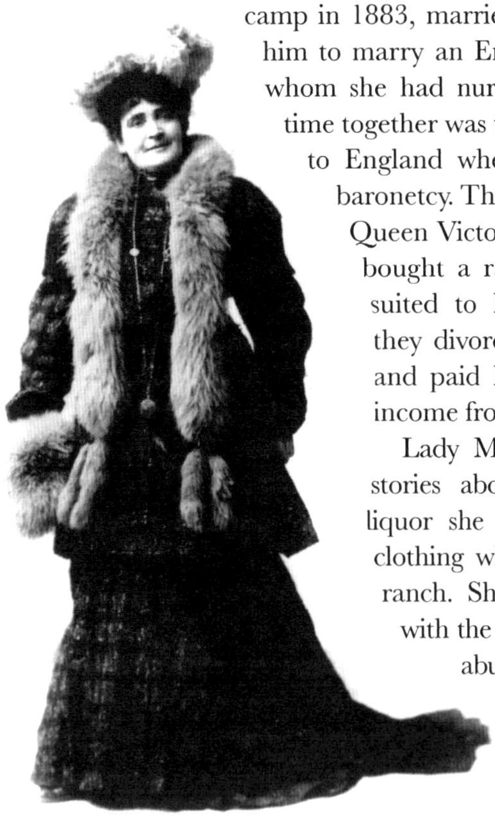

Catherine Moon married an English peer and kept her title after the divorce; she paid her ex-husband alimony. A street in Fort Collins bears her name. *H01514.*

Lady Moon was often seen in town; stories abounded about the bottles of liquor she concealed in her voluminous clothing when she came down from her ranch. She could ride, herd and shoot with the best of the cowboys; she drank abundantly and, it was said, cursed freely, but she was loved by many for her kind heart and generous nature. She often took in strays—people and animals—and helped her friends when she could. Moon died in 1926.

Though the nearby mountains did give up some silver, the canyon and surrounding areas did not yield much gold, but the region was rich in timber. Logs, many intended as railroad ties, were floated down the Poudre, and trails were forged, but thus far no roads had been built and no track laid. Surveying the canyon, the GSL&P engineers declared the enterprise feasible, but after laying about fifteen miles of track in 1882 and losing many railroad ties in a surprise flood, the company gave up, judging the effort too costly. GSL&P connected Fort Collins to Greeley but failed to cross the continental divide via Poudre Canyon.

More and more, the canyon was becoming integral to the life and culture of the town as a place to recreate, a source of lumber, a fishing site and a promising place to homestead. One intrepid pioneer, John Zimmerman, brought his family to the canyon in 1884 after spending four years in the area as a hunter, prospector and tour guide. They settled in the upper canyon in what became known as Home, Colorado. His wife and four children lived on the homestead near Cameron Pass with no neighbors for about two years. After surviving the severe winter of '84 (with Zimmerman often away hunting), the family moved farther down the canyon, where he began building Keystone Resort, open for fishing, hunting and hiking and a very popular place for several decades. When her parents and siblings died, Agnes Zimmerman hung on valiantly as long as she could, but in her old age she had to finally abandon the resort her father had built by hand, the place where so many happy gatherings were held with those present chatting amiably and listening to Zimmerman play his fiddle. The resort is gone and the land acquired by the State of Colorado.

Along with increasing acculturation, wider educational opportunities and facilities and growing commerce, city services continued to improve. In 1887, Thomas Edison's newly patented arc lamps graced city streets for the first time, thanks to William Miner, a local sheep farmer; E.T. Dunning; W.B. Stewart; and E.P. Roberts, who incorporated the Fort Collins Light and Power Company. A newspaper article years later speculated that Miner might have become excited about electricity when he saw bright arc lights used by a traveling circus; author John De Haes calls this as good an explanation as any for what motivated Miner. Gradually, businesses and homeowners began subscribing to this new service. Early records show, according to De Haes, that meters were often placed in bathrooms, sometimes necessitating a wait on the part of the meter reader, and wires were simply stapled to walls.

Electricity was soon to play a major role in the city's history. In 1887, voters approved $40,000 to build a new courthouse, to be erected on the block between Mountain Avenue and Oak, Mason and Howes Streets. While the courthouse was still under construction, Fort Collins's most infamous murder occurred.

James Howe, normally a well-behaved citizen when sober, became violent when in his cups. On April 4, 1888, Howe entered the couple's home on Walnut Street to find his wife packing to leave him. She ran out of the house, screaming for help. He followed, easily caught her thanks to his longer legs, grabbed her hair and dragged her down to the sidewalk, whereupon he slit her throat in full view of bystanders. While some people ran to aid the wounded woman, who quickly bled to death, a group of men surrounded Howe and took him to the sheriff, whereupon he was clapped in jail.

That night, the newly lighted town was suddenly plunged into darkness again. A mob of determined men broke into the jail and hauled Howe out. Though he pleaded for mercy, he was dragged to the site of the courthouse and strung up on a derrick being used in the construction, where he was hanged by the neck until dead.

Legend has it that the town's best-known African American resident, Charlie Clay, sat atop the derrick and played his harmonica while Howe swung. When it was determined the murderer had finally expired, the lights in town mysteriously came on again. Western-style justice had prevailed with no interference from law enforcement.

Clay was a slave who bought his freedom for $600 and came west around 1850. He variously worked as a cook, barber and deliveryman. During Fort Collins's early years, African Americans were few in number in the West, but Clay was one who was able to live here in peace and independence. Over time, he became a much-loved town "character" known for his tall tales. One of them was about a battle he had with Native Americans during which he barricaded himself behind a covered wagon and fought desperately for his life. He also spoke, with a chuckle, about the time General Ulysses S. Grant stopped in Laporte during a western tour. Clay, an accomplished cook, baked an apple pie, which he set on a windowsill to cool while awaiting the general's arrival. Though the general enjoyed a sumptuous meal prepared by Clay, he did not have pie for dessert, for someone had absconded with it while it was cooling on the sill. (Some accounts of this event assert that the delicacy was a dish of potatoes.) In his later years, Clay became the town trash collector.

Back when the fort was still in operation, a grave site had been set aside for soldiers who died in the line of duty or from wounds or disease. At the southwest corner of what became College Avenue and Oak Street, their bodies were laid

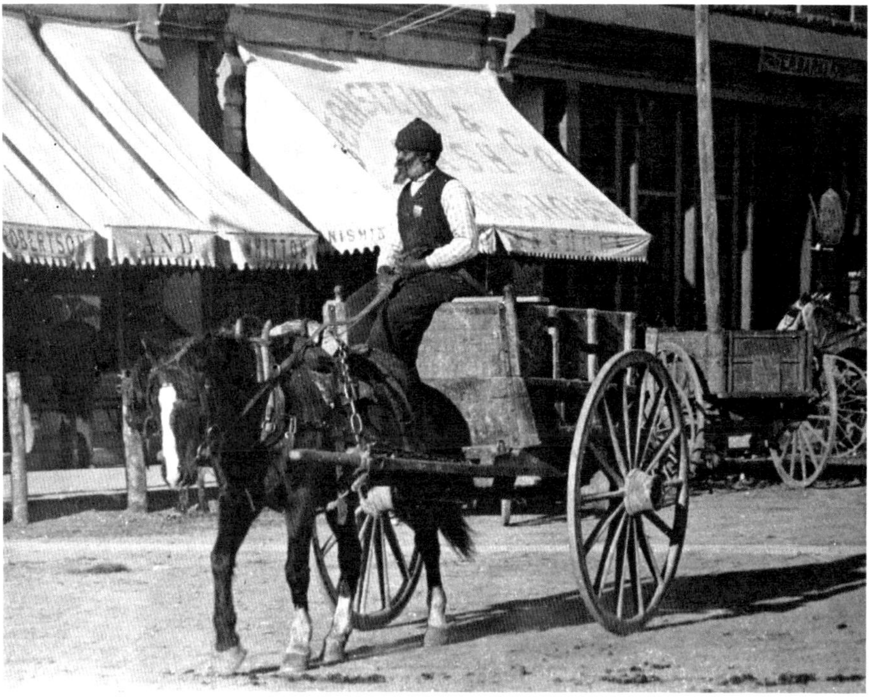

This photograph of Charlie Clay on his refuse wagon is the only known image of this affable, multitalented man who cooked, cut hair, wrangled cows and fought in the Indian wars. *H00046*.

to rest. But when the town was platted, the grave site was right in the center, so the bodies were carefully moved to Mountain Home Cemetery east of town, considered at the time to be far enough out of town that the deceased could lie undisturbed. Not so. As the town grew, the area around Stover and Elizabeth Streets, just west of the second cemetery, was filling in, so once again a new cemetery was needed. In 1887, the town purchased forty acres from Thomas Connelly for fifty dollars an acre and established Grandview Cemetery at the western end of Mountain Avenue and Oak Street. This cemetery, though now surrounded by the city, remains much as it was more than one hundred years ago. (Several years ago, workers digging a new basement on Eastdale Drive discovered bones from Mountain Home Cemetery, which were subsequently buried with honors in Grandview.)

Connelly's land had once been part of the Mercer Colony, which had been started in 1869 by emigrants from Mercer County, Pennsylvania. The group, led by the Reverend W.T. McAdams, chose land on what would later become Prospect Park and began digging a ditch to have a water supply. The settlers ran out of funds and, within a decade, had sold the land to John Sheldon, who farmed it. According to Watrous, the only resident of the colony who stayed in Fort Collins was Alfred Edwards.

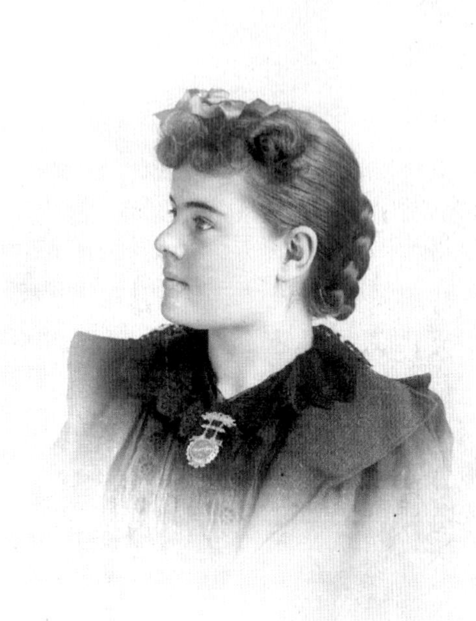

A veteran, grocer and photographer, Stephen Seckner took this sepia photograph of Fanny Cunningham sometime in the late nineteenth century. The serious pose was quite typical of the times. *Courtesy of Danny Rogers.*

Despite all the progress in so many ways, and all the positive signs of growth, one area of major concern remained unsolvable: disease prevention. Physicians at the time had few means of preventing or combatting infections. The vast medical knowledge that unfolded in the next century was yet to come; the germ theory of disease was slow to be accepted. Doctors still had few effective means of relieving pain. Because of the state of medical knowledge at the time, the appearance of disease was not then connected to unsanitary water, and sanitization of instruments was not a common practice. Yet the majority of people were strong and healthy, toughened to the exigencies that buffeted them.

A visitor to the town during this time might be more pleased than repulsed, as Isabella Bird had been when the town was just beginning. That visitor would find a town with clean, modern hotels; a variety of business establishments; churches; progressive schools; a ready source of water; electricity; and even the telephone, along with a railroad line right through the center of town. Our visitor would surely have been favorably impressed.

Chapter 6

During the Growth Years

Optimism

Fire, a hazard that had plagued the town since its beginnings, scorched Poudre Canyon in 1893. It had been a very dry summer, and the timber and brush were unresisting to the mammoth flames. All anyone could do, says Norman Fry in his book about Poudre Canyon, was get out of the way. They had no way to stop the fire; it burned for weeks. People in town began to worry about how far it would—could—go. At last, in July, rain came, putting out the fire and leaving nothing but "blackened waste." The ruined trees with their scorched trunks stretched skyward in mute testimony to the devastation. In time, the forest regenerated itself, as forests will, causing Fry to comment, "Nature is a wonderful rebuilder."

Although no technology had existed to enable mere humans to extinguish that memorable blaze, as the new century approached, technological advances were tumbling over one another. The railroad alone had wrought enormous changes in the world; the harnessing of electric power, improved communications via the telephone and telegraph and increasing industrialization were inexorably altering the United States, up until then a primarily agrarian society. What was happening in the country, in the world, was happening in Fort Collins, too.

Perhaps the last decade of the nineteenth century is most remembered here because of what happened in 1895, when the WCTU at last succeeded in bringing an end to the serving of liquor in Fort Collins, an ordinance that was to last more than seventy years. One catalyst for the passing of this ordinance was the tragedy of a man who had drunk too much, fallen on the sidewalk and frozen to death. Another factor was almost certainly the fact that women in Colorado now had the vote. Famed suffragette Carrie Chapman Catt had come to the Opera House that year seeking support for a nationwide vote for women. Catt was a founder of the League of Women Voters, which had a chapter in Fort Collins by 1920.

Alice Edwards, an anti–liquor license candidate, was elected alderman. Women went to the polls, and as a result, prohibition was in and liquor sales were out. The expiration of Frank Miller's saloon license in 1896 spelled the end of liquor sales for decades to come.

Auntie Stone, whose long life ended in 1895, was able to vote for the first time in her life—she was a strong supporter of temperance. In April 1894, wheelchair-bound, she was wheeled by her son to the polls for a local election. When she died, church bells tolled out each of her ninety-four years. "All business in the city was suspended" during her funeral, Watrous reports.

The woman who had so influenced the town's early history died in an era of considerable change and some controversy in Fort Collins. With the town becoming more mature and urban, differences arose on campus about what the focus of the college should be. As a land grant institution, its primary mission was agricultural education and research. However, there were those who advocated broadening the curriculum to include more liberal arts and humanities. Resistant to these changes, the school continued its agricultural emphasis but did expand offerings to include more courses in domestic arts, science and the humanities. The societal roles of men and women were still being clearly delineated.

The gap between town and gown continued unabated, with local residents very aware of the economic advantages of having the college here but not entirely trusting toward academia in general and the faculty and staff at the college turning more inward than outward. Downtown merchants, interested in protecting their turf, were reluctant to cater to the needs of the school, and students, who were still required to work on campus, tended to keep their noses to the grindstone, as it were.

Residents of the town also wanted wider opportunities to expand their interests and knowledge. A group of WCTU members and other women organized a public library, which was housed in the Welch Block, in 1899. The idea of public libraries, free to anyone who wanted to borrow a book and supported by taxpayers, was new on the cultural horizon. Prior to this energetic, progressive era, libraries had been mostly maintained in private homes or, in some cases, in a public space but accessible only to subscribers who paid a fee. In Fort Collins, the library group acquired about eight hundred books, many of them donated by the Reverend George Falconer of Unity Church, to start their public library with hopes of more books being donated, since they had no budget for purchasing books. Within a short time, a city library association was formed, the city took possession of the collection and the books were moved to an available room on College Avenue. Thus, the first free public library sanctioned by the city was official before the turn of the century.

The year 1899 saw another noteworthy event. George Glover, the shy teen who had come to the school two decades earlier, had obtained a degree in veterinary medicine from Iowa State College and returned to the faculty at Colorado Agricultural College (CAC). Due in part to the efforts of the Stockmen's Association, the college expanded its studies in veterinary medicine under Glover's leadership.

Earlier, in 1893, the college had also experienced a different kind of "first": a football team. The first game for CAC found the team facing off against Longmont Academy on January 7, 1893, in Longmont. In its infancy, football was an elemental sport, with no rules of play and much scrapping. The players might have worn nose guards, but such protective gear as helmets and padding was in the future. Referees were unofficial volunteers. The average weight of the players, according to Hansen, was 165 pounds. Injuries were common; in every game, at least two or three players were carried off the field. Emerging the losers from their first contest, the CAC team sustained only two serious injuries: one broken rib and one sprained knee.

Although not sanctioned by the college administration, the team continued to play through the winter, meeting Longmont again (winning this time) and Normal School in Greeley (now the University of Northern Colorado) and, disastrously, losing 70–6 to the University of Colorado in Boulder, a keen competition that continues to this day.

On one occasion CAC's opponents, losing badly, brought in a ringer—a 250-pound railroad hand who happened to have been watching the game. (Bringing in outsiders was an ongoing problem then.) No players were taken off the field to make room for him, so the CAC team was outnumbered and outweighed—but won anyway.

The president of the college, Alston Ellis, felt that football promoted "senseless brutality," says Hansen, and was unnecessary to the course of education, so he banned the practice. No sanctioned football was played on the CAC campus until a changing of the guard in 1899, when the new president, Barton Aylesworth, once again allowed the sport.

Football for some, cycling for others. The sport and art of riding a bicycle gained rapidly in popularity in the years before 1900. By 1890, the unwieldy penny farthing bicycle, with its high front wheel, small back wheel and cumbersome pedaling (vividly described in a tongue-in-cheek Twain essay), had been replaced by a "safety bicycle," chain-driven with more level wheels, pneumatic tires and pedals in the middle. Women could easily and safely ride these bicycles (often over the vociferous objections of men). Susan B. Anthony heralded the arrival of the bicycle as a great emancipator of women, for in order to ride a bicycle, they had to discard their heavy, corseted dresses in favor of bloomers, which were much more comfortable—and safer. In Fort Collins, cycling became very popular during the "bicycle craze" years, leading to an ordinance prohibiting bicycle riding on sidewalks but failing to discourage riding by both sexes elsewhere. Women formed riding clubs to enjoy outings together. (Today, many residents of Fort Collins of both genders get around on bicycles.)

Others on campus and in the community enjoyed a more intellectual diversion: debate. Frequently, debates on all kinds of topics, national or very local, were held in the auditorium of Old Main, bringing in lively and participatory crowds. Debate clubs were popular, and finely tuned rhetoric was prized by many. The classic rules of debate applied, and decorum was observed by the debaters. While a student at the college, Elizabeth Coy, daughter of John and Emily Coy, won a debate.

Progress in industry and technology continued apace. By the 1890s, more than fifty people had subscribed to the telephone service, with headquarters in a local drugstore, and as medical knowledge expanded, more doctors set up shop here. The time for a community hospital was approaching, but some private hospitals preceded it.

In 1893, a retired army nurse, Christian White, began offering nursing care in his home. Though not noted as the first hospital, his was the first effort here for a facility providing medical care to the public. Several doctors were on the scene before 1900—Dr. P.J. McHugh, who came in 1890 and later studied in Vienna; Dr. William Kickland; Dr. E.A. Lee; and Dr. Charles Miller, who had served as county health officer in the 1880s. When Dr. Miller died a few years later, his wife, Nora Rice Miller, went to medical school, obtained a license and practiced medicine here for several years. Though her patients were mostly women, her practice thrived.

Dr. Timothy Smith, the town's first doctor, had left Fort Collins by 1882, though not before fathering twins in his seventies. He and his family had survived the Welch Block fire. His remaining colleagues were kept busy going all over the area treating patients, delivering babies and dispensing medications.

All vestiges of the Wild West now gone from the civilized frontier town, the residents might expect law and order to prevail—which they did, most of the time. But in 1891, one of the century's most sensational murder trials took place in the aftermath of the untimely death of William Avery, brother of Franklin Avery. William, unexpectedly dead of a presumed stomach ailment, was laid to rest with no suspicion attached to his demise until his newly widowed wife remarried just twelve days after his death. The man she married, Frank Millington, had once been Avery's business partner. Suspicion fell on Mary, Frank and Frank's sister, Dillie, and they were arrested. The ensuing trial was considered too prejudicial to be held here, so it was moved to Denver. Ultimately, the accused were acquitted, some said thanks to the heartrending testimony of the Averys' daughter, Pearl, who tearfully professed her mother's innocence.

Avery, the prosecution claimed, was worth a great deal of money, which Mary would inherit. The friendship between Mary and Frank, the defense countered, was entirely above board before Avery's death, and Pearl verified the platonic nature of their relationship. Franklin Avery, convinced his younger brother had been murdered, spent a considerable sum of his own money to aid prosecutors—to no avail. Although arsenic was found in his body when William Avery's remains were exhumed, the prosecution could not establish beyond a reasonable doubt that Mary had somehow served the poison to her husband. The all-male jury was apparently not inclined to convict a pretty young woman on the evidence provided to it.

Mary, Pearl and Frank left Fort Collins, never to return.

Leaving aside this local sensation, life for the most part at this time was peaceful and prosperous. Lamb feeding was coming into wider use among local ranchers, especially after a trainload of sheep, stranded in Trinidad, Colorado, by a blizzard, was eventually relocated to Fort Collins, where alfalfa was plentiful. The surviving lambs thrived and grew, and the profitability of the enterprise attracted entrepreneurs. Lamb feeding was to be important in the area for several more years.

Partly as a result of experiments with plants performed by the Agricultural Extension Service, sugar beet farming began in earnest around 1890. The experiments proved that the soil and climate in the area were ideal for growing the beets, and it was soon discovered that the beet tops and pulp were useful for feeding livestock. The industry would attract a large number of Germans from Russia, emigrating after the terms of their stay in Russia had

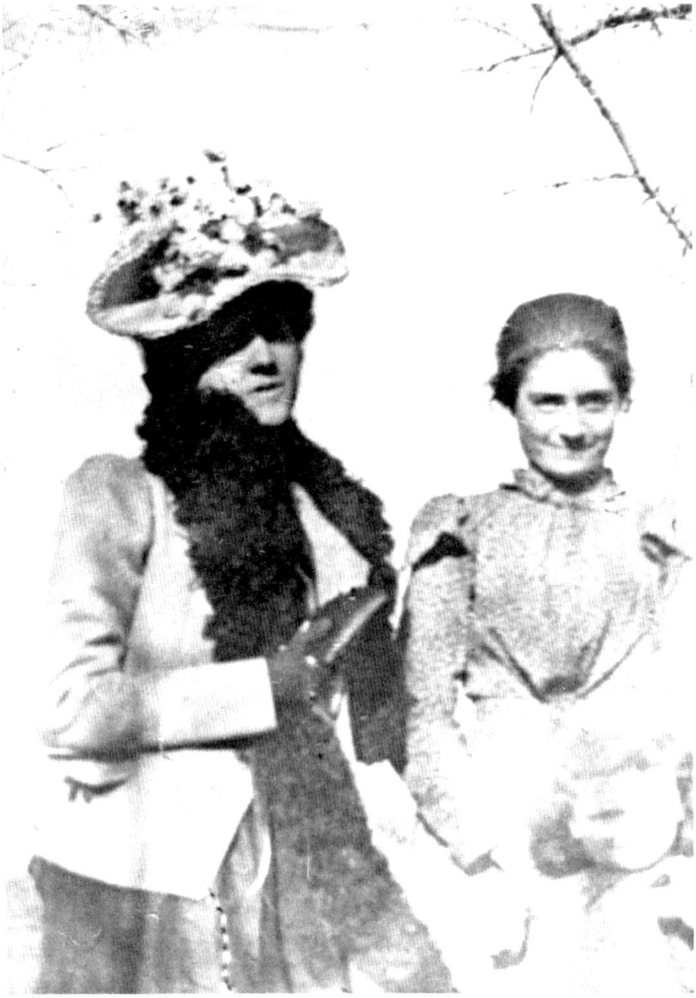

As a young girl, Pearl Avery (left) tearfully testified to her mother's innocence when Mary Avery was on trial for murdering her husband. The woman on the right is Aurelia Bouton. *H07457.*

changed. Farmers, these immigrants knew beet growing exceptionally well. The industry would also prove highly profitable for processors of the beets.

Both of these enterprises reinforced the agrarian nature of business and industry in Fort Collins; the college remained primarily focused on practical studies. The town grew, becoming a vibrant Northern Colorado center of commerce and industry. Residents looked forward to the new century with optimism—for good reason.

Chapter 7

Into the New Century

CHANGE

While the people of Fort Collins eagerly anticipated the arrival of a new century, which promised to be full of technological advances and improvements in the quality of life, they could not have had any inkling of what the 1900s would bring to Fort Collins and to the world. It was not just change that would happen, but seismic change—enormous upheaval that would, ultimately, completely overturn the world they had known.

This world, so familiar and comfortable, moved at a relatively slow pace. The horse still transported people and goods, pulled plows and, with a cowboy in the saddle, helped ranchers manage their herds. Bicyclists in the roadway did not fear being knocked down or forced off the road. Women mainly stayed in the home, raising children (though this had been slowly changing for some time); suffragettes continued to agitate for nationwide votes for women. Men were in charge of the town, of commerce, of industry and of politics. Men were also in charge of the college; a few women had joined the faculty, but they were distinctly outnumbered. Constrained by their clothing (except those who dared to wear bloomers), few women took part in athletic events or competitions.

One potential resident, Joe Alpert, who had fled from a pogrom in Russia during which his grandparents were killed before his eyes while he hid from the soldiers, chose Fort Collins to raise his family in part because it was liquor-free. He also liked the prospect of a college education for his children and employment for himself at the sugar beet factory. To him, the town looked like a placid, comfortable place to settle and, he hoped, to cure his wife's asthma.

Certainly, Alpert was correct in that the unavailability of liquor in town and the proliferation of churches contributed to a relatively sedate and well-behaved populace, but liquor was available for those who knew where to find it (for years, drugstores sold "medicinal" concoctions known to contain alcohol perfectly legally), and "ladies of the night" could be found by those who knew where to look. The WCTU had accomplished its goal of a liquor-free town. Yet the result was—as happens so often—unintended consequences.

For one, there was "the jungle," an area in the vicinity of Vine Drive that was just outside the city limits and a hotbed of all kinds of activity, much of it illegal. For another, there was Stout.

The quarry at Stout, a few miles west of town, was still active in 1900, even though concrete was beginning to replace stone for sidewalks and some construction purposes. Also outside the city limits, Stout was known for its saloons and the consequent barroom brawls, for its houses of ill repute and for its generally freewheeling lifestyle. Men considered perfectly respectable on the streets of Fort Collins could go to Stout to seek entertainments not found in town.

In town, one woman offering such entertainments was largely tolerated despite her questionable reputation. A Frenchwoman, Marie Lafitte (possibly not her real name), had come here in 1899 and promptly set up shop, operating a place on Linden thought by many to be a brothel called the "Kandy Kitchen," where it was known that liquor could be obtained. Though she appeared in court from time to time until her death in 1914, she was often let off lightly, possibly because some of her clients were men of high position in the town, judges among them. Lafitte had a sad life, ending up in court on numerous occasions, more often because of property disputes than because of illegal activities. One attorney in particular took a violent dislike to Madame Lafitte and on one occasion beat her severely. She eventually lost her property, though she fought hard to keep it, and died a pauper, taken by diabetes and burns suffered in a house fire.

Liquor problems surfaced once again in 1903, when the town marshal, William Richart, went to the bottling works owned by Robert Miller because he had been told liquor was being sold there and had secured warrants to search the premises and arrest Miller. Confronted by the marshal, who was accompanied by a night watchman and a deputy sheriff, Miller threw a bottle at the marshal, who responded by firing his weapon at Miller with fatal results. Richart was charged with murder. Accounts of the affair differed at the trial, with Miller's young son, who was a witness, saying that his father had done nothing to provoke the shot and the marshal saying that it was dark in the bottling room, he could not see what Miller was doing and he thought Miller was reaching for a gun so he fired in self-defense. Richart described a scuffle during which Miller came at him. Richart said that when he pulled out his gun, Miller retorted, "To hell with your gun, we are not afraid of it."

In spite of not being able to see much, as he had claimed, the marshal succeeded in striking Miller right in the heart. He died instantly. The all-male jury chose to believe the town marshal and came back with a verdict of not guilty. (Women did not start serving on juries here until after World War II.)

By the turn of the century, medical care had made significant advances, but doctors had difficulty coping when an epidemic of typhoid fever broke out in 1900. More than three hundred people fell ill. Twenty-four people died. In the late nineteenth century, English physicians had postulated that the typhoid bacillus was carried in the bowel waste of those infected and could be transmitted to others through contaminated drinking water. Applying the theory to local water, which came from the river, doctors deduced that somehow the water was being contaminated even though strict instructions about boiling water before use and properly disposing of waste had been publicized widely. An expert from Denver, Dr. William Mitchell, came to assess the situation and discovered that one woman who was caring for a sick relative was dumping the patient's waste into a ditch that emptied right into the river, hence into the city's water supply. Though the epidemic abated in due time, it became clear to city officials that something needed to be done to purify the city's water.

Accordingly, the voters approved the building of a new water plant in 1903. Reported the *Fort Collins Express*, "The people voted to issue municipal bonds of the city to the amount of $150,000, the proceeds of the sales of which to be used in the extension and enlargement of the city's water system." The water would be delivered by a gravity system, providing four million gallons of water every twenty-four hours. The new plant was constructed at the base of the canyon, in a place now known as Gateway Park. The first plant on Overland Trail would lie idle, deteriorating, until restoration began nearly a century later.

It would, however, take six more years to address the problem of pure water. In 1909, the city had installed a mechanical filter to purify the water before it reached its users. Later, even more sophisticated filters were installed. As the population grew, doubling between 1900 and 1910, the need for not only pure water but also enough of it expanded exponentially. Ditches, some dug as early as 1860, diverted water from the river, so adequate water storage became an ongoing issue, still of concern to the city today.

Dealing with the elderly and indigent motivated the county to build a poor farm and old folks' home in the early 1900s on land east of town that had once been a fairground. The residents planted and tended a garden, cared for livestock, milked cows, did their own laundry and prepared their own meals. The county had purchased the land in order to eventually build a hospital there; in the meantime, the poor farm served as a hospital. Though it had an operating room, it was poorly equipped, says author Dr. Stanley Hensen, and the facility had no laboratory. Dr. A.W. Kilgore was appointed county physician. Nurses were paid about thirty dollars a month, with room and board provided but no guaranteed time off, so they went to town when they could get away.

Coming together to address health concerns in the wake of the epidemic, several local doctors cooperated to form the Fort Collins Hospital Association with the goal of building a modern facility open to the public, as opposed to the private hospitals offering care at the time, that would also provide a safe, sanitary location for surgery. Many advances had been made in surgical procedures in the last few years. Kickland and McHugh were eager to have a suitable place to operate. The Fort Collins Hospital, at the southeast corner of Mulberry and Magnolia Streets, opened in 1906. Doctors had stock in the venture, so it remained a private hospital, but the newspapers were impressed: electric lighting, heat and plumbing were installed, along with a laboratory; the walls were painted a cheerful yellow and nurses were on hand to tend to patients. The building could accommodate about forty patients but had no special area set off for childbirth or children. That building, now a private residence, still stands.

One story often told about the hospital said that patients who could not walk up stairs had to be raised and lowered to the upper floor on a door outside of the building, the stairways being too unwieldy.

The physicians soon opened a training school for nurses, teaching the courses themselves. The nurses also served as housekeepers and did various chores around the hospital in addition to caring for patients. Nursing was making progress toward the respected profession it is today, but there was still a ways to go.

Although progress and innovation were happening very fast here and elsewhere in the first years of the new century, there was still the risk of flooding because of too much rain or snowmelt. A significant flood in 1864 had resulted in the establishment of Fort Collins. In 1904, the river spoke again. The rains began on May 20, 1904, almost forty years to the day after the Laporte flood. Soon, the bottomland near the river was full of water. Residents in low-lying areas along the river were driven out of their homes. Some saw everything they owned float away.

Living in a homestead he had established in May 1860, when, according to Watrous, "it can almost be said of a truth that the history of the white settlement of the county began with the advent in its borders of Mr. Strauss on May 15th, 1860," the elderly Robert Strauss found his cabin surrounded by water. Leaving his home, he headed toward a neighbor's, but the rushing water trapped him against a barbed-wire fence, where he clung all night, water swirling around him, calling feebly for help. In the morning, in daylight, the neighbor discovered him, but alas, Strauss had been so chilled

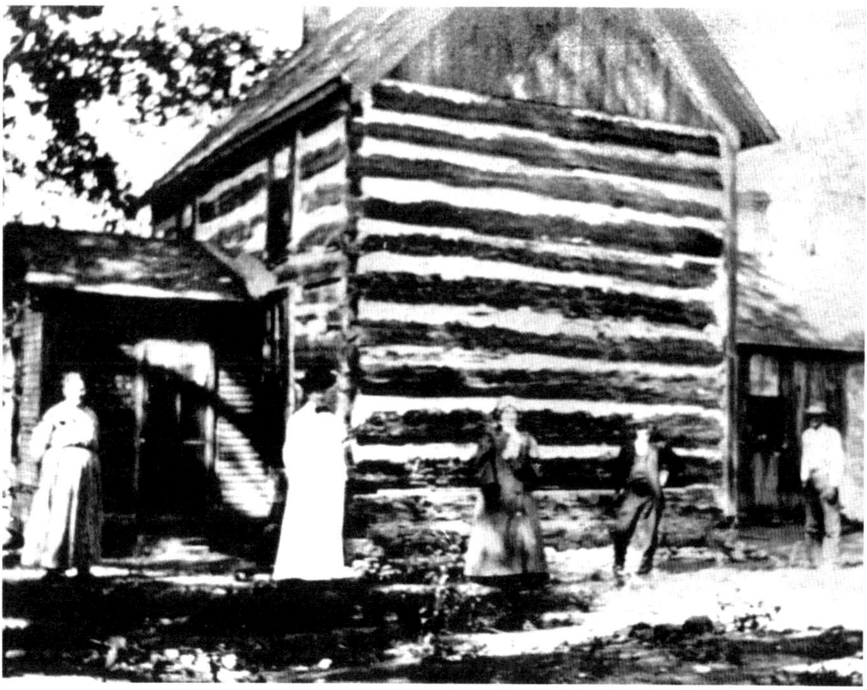

Robert Strauss built his cabin near the Poudre River. It withstood several floods, including the one in 1904 that killed Strauss himself, but was torched by vandals a number of years ago. *H02492.*

by a night in the water that he died a few hours later. The flood of '64 had taken his garden; the flood of '04 took his life.

Watrous honors Strauss as "a specimen of the brave, independent westerners; sanguine in temperament, genial in disposition and honorable in thought and deed…It is to such men as he that his survivors in the valley are greatly indebted."

Though the flood did considerable damage near the river, the land near the new sugar beet factory was hardest hit. Recovery was slow, but the more fortunate residents on higher ground provided clothes and food to those who suffered the most damage, many of them factory and field workers.

The factory had become a reality earlier that year. With financing arranged more quickly, Loveland had beaten Fort Collins in the sugar beet factory race, but local businessmen soon gathered enough money to build a factory here. It was located on the south side of Vine Drive. With guarantees from local farmers of at least five thousand acres of beets to process, the enterprise was soon underway.

Actually a complex of businesses—farmers, laborers, suppliers, beet dump stations, the railroad line and factory workers—the factory pumped a substantial amount of money into the community, vitalizing and sustaining the economy. Workers were brought in to tend and harvest the beets; whole families could often be found in the fields, only the youngest not required to work. *Second Hoeing*, a book published several years later by Hope Sykes, who taught in Fort Collins, describes in graphic detail the life of a beet worker family. Though the factory began as a local private enterprise, it was soon purchased by the Great Western Sugar Company.

Germans from Russia were well established enough here by the early 1900s for the Lutherans among them to erect a stone church, a Fuller design, at the northeast corner of Whedbee and Olive Streets. Congregants hauled stone from the quarry by wagon and built the church stone by stone. Acknowledging both their new country and their German roots, they carved the cornerstone in both English and German. The church is one of the few original ones downtown that still stands and is still used as a church.

Lured to Russia by Empress Catherine the Great with guarantees of free land, freedom of religion, freedom from conscription and free transportation to Russia, German immigrants moved to a new land in the mid-eighteenth century. Herself German born, the empress invited them to settle along the Volga River, hoping to increase the population there and to see more productivity from the land. She knew that Germany was struggling economically and that citizens might be amenable to coming with

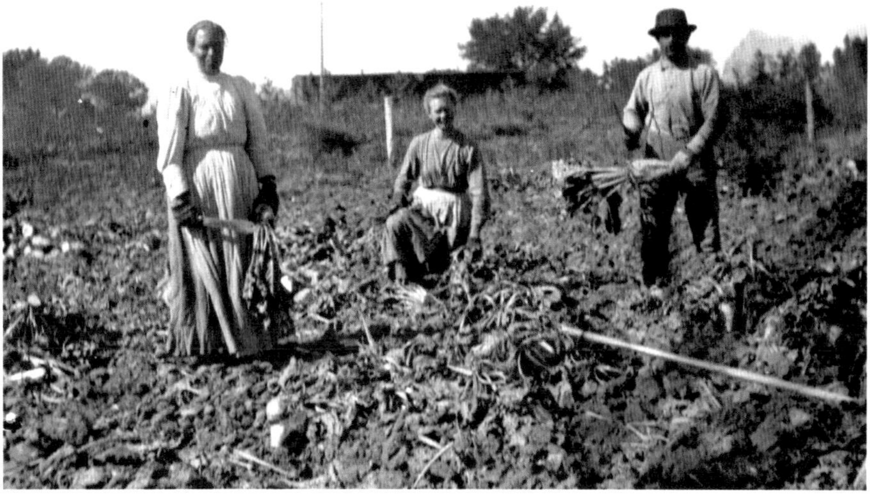

Topping sugar beets was backbreaking work. In this photo, Charlie Hoffman (right) is identified; the others are not. *H05389A.*

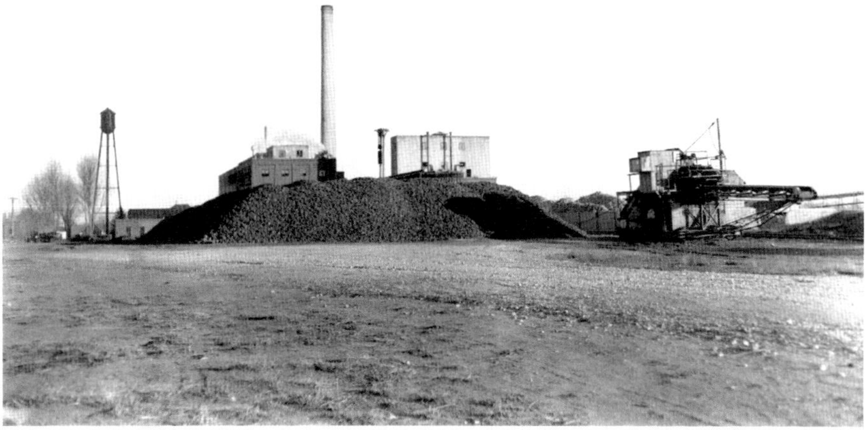

A large pile of harvested sugar beets awaits processing at the Great Western Sugar Factory. *10176H.*

the enticements she offered. These promises were kept until Alexander II, Catherine's great-grandson, came to the throne more than one hundred years later. Suddenly these colonists, who still spoke their native language, found themselves taken for military service and forced to learn Russian—deprivations not to be borne.

Many fled to the United States, settling in the fertile Midwest, first in Dakota Territory and later in Iowa, Nebraska, Kansas and Colorado. The Great Western Sugar Factory brought many of them to the Fort Collins–Loveland area, where they worked in the beet fields and the factory. Homes went up for the workers, twelve- by twelve-foot boxes across from the plant. Andersonville was developed on land owned by Peter Anderson, one of the investors in the factory, in order to provide housing nearby for the factory workers.

The Germans from Russia were not the only builders of churches. In the 300 block of Mountain Avenue a new Catholic church, also of stone, was going up by 1901. The energetic priest who drove the project, Father Guillaume LaJeunesse, had come to Fort Collins in 1899 and immediately set about to acquire land for a church. St. Joseph's Catholic Church was built at the northwest corner of Mountain Avenue and Howes Street. Under his guidance, a rectory next to the church and a parochial school, St. Joseph's Catholic School across Howes Street, went up in the next few years. St. Joseph's is another surviving downtown church still in use as a church, still by the same denomination.

In 1905, Unity Church (Unitarian) built a church at the southwest corner of College Avenue and Mulberry Street, and in 1907, the First United Presbyterian Church built at the corner of Mathews and Mulberry Streets. Both of these edifices are gone today.

A newly renovated hotel enhanced downtown architecture in 1904. A consortium of businessman bought the Commercial Hotel at the corner of Walnut Street and College Avenue, renovating it, adding a floor and renaming it the Northern. Newspapers labeled it "the pearl of Northern Colorado" and marveled at its magnificence and modernity. Close to the railroad station, it attracted many guests for its eighty rooms. The large dining room featured a leaded dome in the ceiling. Across the street the Orpheum Theater opened a few years later and offered another amazing innovation of the new century: moving pictures. However, movies were not often on hand, so live entertainment was the usual fare. College Avenue and environs were lively with activity.

Commercial buildings and stately homes were being constructed, a sure sign of prosperity. Then in 1906, Fort Collins joined the modern age by

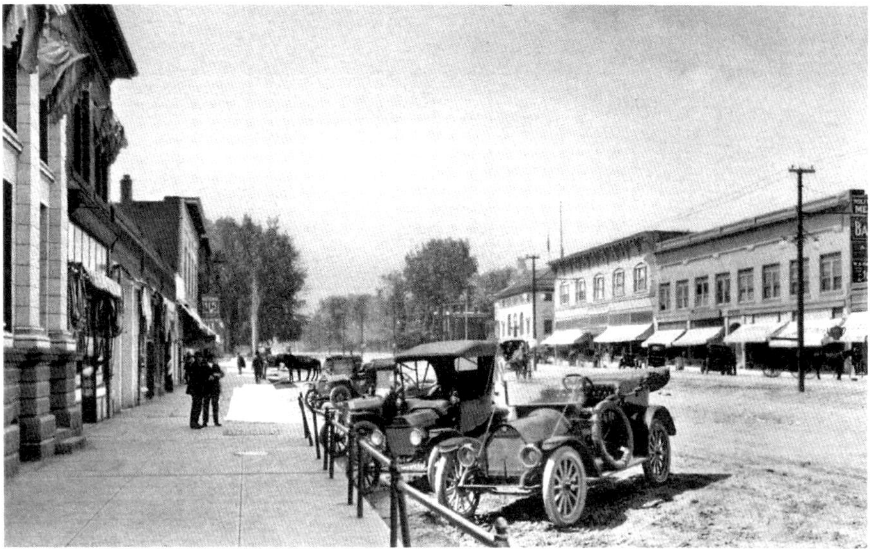

Not long after the arrival of the automobile in Fort Collins, South College Avenue had room for both motorized and horse-drawn vehicles. *Courtesy of Malcolm McNeill.*

contracting with the Denver and Interurban Company to provide trolley service, which came on line in 1907. The cars were large, heavy, lumbering vehicles with a cowcatcher in front. Traffic was chaotic in the early 1900s; drivers generally stayed right but sometimes veered into the middle of the street. Horse-drawn wagons occasionally had unfortunate encounters with streetcars and with the automobiles beginning to appear on the streets. Pity the poor pedestrian, who all along had to dodge horses and their leavings and now had the added hazards of streetcars and autos. Like most small towns of that time, Fort Collins was mainly a walking town coming into the twentieth century. All that changed in the early 1900s, with dizzying speed.

Along with the streetcars came the automobile, that newfangled invention that captured the imagination of the populace in almost no time at all. In fact, the automobile arrived in town before the streetcar.

In his book *The Automobile Comes to Fort Collins*, Malcolm McNeill describes the arrival, in 1902, of the first car, a curved-dash Oldsmobile driven by Judge J. Mack Mills. The judge took the train to Denver to purchase his car for $700 and then drove it back to his home in Fort Collins, arriving, his daughter said, looking like a mud statue.

Picture the automobile, circa 1902: It was open to the elements, with the steering device on the right. No windshield, no bumpers, no fenders.

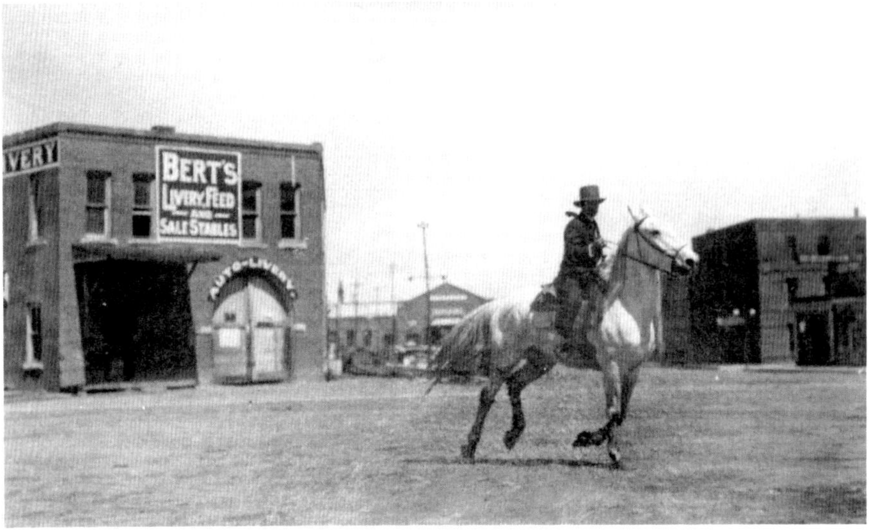

Note the sign over the arched doorway that indicates he is also prepared to serve customers with automobiles. Bert's Livery and Stables would not be in business much longer. *Courtesy of Malcolm McNeill.*

Hand cranking to start it could be hazardous—drivers sometimes suffered broken bones. Brass sidelights were intended to make night driving easier. The engine, located under the single seat, was smaller than that of a contemporary riding mower. The car weighed about 650 pounds.

Now imagine the roads of that time. No road went directly from Denver to Fort Collins; rather, the roads took a circuitous route through Greeley and Berthoud—in essence, the stagecoach line. No directional or regulatory signs or lane markers aided drivers. There was no such thing as a traffic light, no rules of the road. Cars, which truly were "horseless carriages" then because they were built like motorized carriages, had to follow stagecoach ruts.

Consider the driver. Mills drove the car around a little with the dealer on board—that was his driving lesson and about as much as any driver got in those days. No license was required, and no age limits were imposed. Once, Mills's young daughter, Freda, took the wheel on the hills during a drive to Estes Park, a fifty-six-mile trip following the stage route through Lyons. Her father ran behind to prevent the car from rolling backward, carrying two big rocks to put under the rear wheels if that were to happen.

These early cars did not go very fast—the Olds went about ten miles an hour on good roads. After he had bought the car, Mills spent the night in Berthoud before heading home. It had rained that day, and he had no protection—thus his dramatic but triumphant mud-covered arrival. Later, when Mills took a trip to Berthoud, a local newspaper congratulated him for making such good time—an hour and five minutes to go twenty miles.

Despite the cataclysmic advent of the automobile, which many saw as a rich man's toy and quite unlikely to overtake the horse anytime soon, horses remained a central part of life in the town in the early 1900s, and interest in horse racing was high. In 1904, Fred Sherwood bought farmland west of town owned by John Sheldon, formed the Gentlemen's Riding and Driving Club and opened Prospect Park, a popular venue for horse racing where harness and buggy races ("gentlemen's races") were held.

In 1907, acting on a petition submitted to the city council for recreational facilities, the city purchased Sheldon's land, which had been part of the original and short-lived Mercer Colony decades earlier, for about $28,000. By 1913, with grading and other work complete, the city added Prospect Park to the sixty-two acres first purchased to complete the park acreage. Soon, the area became a popular recreation spot, thanks to Sheldon Lake and ample space for recreation.

It was not the only opportunity for recreation—by 1909, Fort Collins had a professional baseball team, and Chautauquas, educational summer traveling tours, were held in town. On one such occasion, William Jennings Bryan, "the golden-tongued orator," lectured here, speaking about the "lust for gain" as the root of evil in the world.

Those who could afford them continued to enjoy their particular form of recreation: the automobile. The inexorable march of the automobile continued; it did not take long before more autos arrived. As has been observed, the vehicles were expensive, beyond the means of the average citizen, so local purchasers were doctors, lawyers and other professionals with higher incomes. One of the earliest purchasers was Dr. William Kickland, who had been enchanted by the speed with which Mills conveyed him to the rural home of a boy with a broken arm. Kickland was soon the owner of the second car in Fort Collins, another Olds.

Women, too, mastered the art of maneuvering automobiles (just as they had mastered the bicycle), another startling change for the times. Despite male doubts about their ability to handle an automobile safely, women saw the new invention as yet another gate to independence, as well as a way to further establish their competence. It did not take long for designers to come up with hats and coverings designed especially for women, both as passengers and as drivers in the open cars. Electric cars were becoming popular as well; both Mrs. A.W. Scott and Mrs. Frank Stover were known

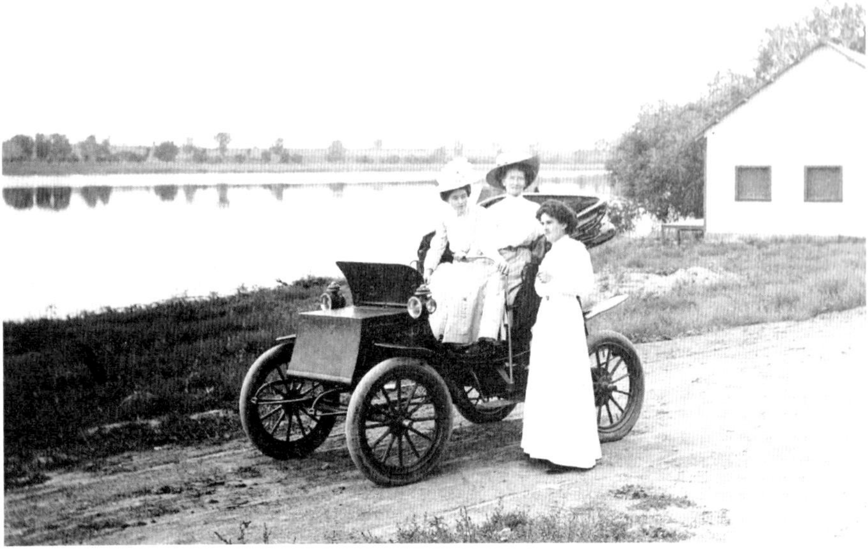

Women were delighted with the arrival of the electric car. Here, the driver might be Mrs. A.W. Scott, and the woman standing might be Mrs. Frank Stover. *Courtesy of Malcolm McNeill.*

to have driven electrics. (The journalistic style at the time, which continued well into the new century, was to identify married women by their husbands' given names rather than their own.)

Also coming into vogue was the Stanley Steamer, popular because of its power but dangerous because lighting a fire was required to start it. Freelan O. Stanley had come to Estes Park in the early 1900s and was so taken with the area that he built a resort hotel there, a building still standing and still open as a hotel and resort. He and his twin brother, Francis, developed the steam autos and sold them quite successfully until the internal combustion engine overtook every other kind of car about ten years after the century had turned. Judge Mills was among Fort Collins residents who purchased a steamer; John Zimmerman used them as shuttles to get guests to his Poudre Canyon Keystone Hotel.

Whatever the make and nature of the automobile, this new mode of transport was coming, rapidly and irrevocably, bringing with it one of the most dramatic changes in the history of human transportation—almost surely the most life-changing. Citizens of Fort Collins who lived during the arrival of the automobile undoubtedly did not envision the enormity of its impact at the time, but all were affected by the change.

Traffic at this time was a sort of organized chaos, with people doing their best to be courteous most of the time. Early in the century, the council saw the necessity for some regulation of automobiles and decreed a speed limit of twelve miles per hour, eight miles per hour going around a corner. There was no way to measure speed, so enforcement of this law was not an exact science.

But for the most part, the majority of Fort Collins citizens were law abiding, and by 1908, there was a police force in place. Though exact records are murky, according to author Tom McLellan, in that year the city marshal was first referred to and considered the chief of police, and there was a force of constables.

Even before that recognition by the city council, law and order were maintained by the city marshal and constables, or policemen. One of them, Joseph Allen, was brutally killed in the jungle in 1907. An area known to have problems with crime from time to time, where liquor was available in what were referred to as "dives," the jungle attracted people who sometimes did not choose to be law-abiding. Allen, who was said to have a wife and family in Kansas, came to Fort Collins on a bicycle, according to historian Rose Brinks, found a job in the police department and soon liked to claim that he knew people in the jungle and could deal with problems there. Unfortunately, on the night of July 3, his luck ran out.

Allen was ambushed as he strolled along on his beat. There were numerous large cottonwood trees in the area at that time, and his assailant evidently concealed himself behind one or behind some bushes, jumping out to attack Allen from behind. There is evidence that Allen tried to defend himself, but the assault was so sudden and unexpected that he could not. He was hit in the head repeatedly, probably with a brick. Moaning and unconscious when found, he died at the hospital a few hours later.

One newspaper account indicates that Allen had once been a Pinkerton man, serving with the detective agency founded just before the Civil War. He later served in the army in Cuba and the Philippines. He was only in his late forties when he was killed. A jury was empaneled to investigate the incident and determined, after viewing the body, that Allen had died from several blows to the head.

Although the police appealed to the public to help solve this terrible crime, and two men were subsequently arrested, no charges were brought, and no one came forward with information. The murder appeared to have been planned, for it was known that Allen did his rounds nightly in that area. Allen's revolver, club and knife had been taken. City officials, businessmen and citizens were aroused and angered by the murder, some vowing to get rid of the jungle, labeled "a plague spot" by Watrous, altogether. Others were deeply concerned about the city's reputation as a law-abiding community.

In time, the jungle changed, and other events diverted attention. Most people forgot after a while—but the police have not. The Allen murder remains an open case in the Fort Collins Police Department files. A street immediately west of the police station honors his memory.

The murder shocked the public, most of whom related it directly to the illegal sale of liquor; such problems certainly arose from time to time. Unwise consumption of liquor led to another murder in 1904 in the town of Stout. Local sentiment was against William Town, who had been arrested for killing William Gardner, a respected family man. Shortly after the arrest, a lynch mob gathered. "The rope and the tree were ready," reported the *Weekly Courier*. But Deputy Sheriff William Richart, warned of the situation, diverted his prisoner away from Laporte until the mob cooled off.

Premeditated murder or self-defense? That's what the jury had to decide. "Toughy" Town confessed to fatally shooting Gardner when both were inebriated. Both workers at the Stout quarry west of town, they had been drinking heavily on the afternoon of February 9, 1904. Claiming it wasn't loaded, Gardner brandished a pistol, which Town somehow took from him. Gardner stepped outside to retrieve his weapon. Town's father, Curtis Town, turned a gun on Gardner and told him to put his hands up. Gardner complied. Young William appeared with a Winchester rifle, which he pointed at Gardner, who said, "Don't shoot."

Barbara Rims, mother of quarry supervisor Thomas Griffith, echoed Gardner's plea. But Town ignored her and fired several times, hitting Gardner in the lung. Three hours later, he died of his wounds.

Evidence against Town was strong. The most damaging testimony came from eleven-year-old Lettie Griffith, who explained that she would never lie because if she did, she knew she would "burn in hell." She reported seeing Town ruthlessly shoot an *unarmed* man, a key issue for the jury.

When Town took the stand, women were cleared from the courtroom, his testimony deemed unfit for their ears. He claimed that Gardner had used foul language and hit him with a bottle—or was it a club? He'd been too drunk to recall clearly. He said Gardner had grabbed him by the throat; he had to defend himself. However, several people had seen Curtis Town hold Gardner at gunpoint until his son had his Winchester rifle in hand, thereby contradicting Town's self-defense claim.

On March 16, the jury returned its verdict: guilty of first-degree murder. Reported the *Courier*, "The jury first went 7–5 for hanging then decided on life in prison." Town appeared relieved, preferring the "gloomy walls of the penitentiary" to the "trap and black cap, pinioned arms and legs. Hardened by crime as the young man is, yet he loves life." That "crime-hardened" lad was eighteen years old.

Without doubt, the town of Stout was a burr in the saddle of the solid citizens of Fort Collins. By the middle of the first decade of the new century, however, activity at the quarry had diminished considerably, Union Pacific having given up its interest in the enterprise. With significantly fewer workers housed in the town, it became less of a magnet for activities considered unacceptable by townspeople.

An action by George Glover brought the town's attention back to the college. For years, he had been lobbying the state Board of Agriculture to support an accredited department of veterinary medicine at the college. The board, however, was reluctant to make the commitment. So Glover made a drastic move. Tuberculosis had surfaced among some cows in the area. Glover invited some members from the board to view a demonstration, a scene graphically described by Hansen. Examining the college's herd for disease, he had found several animals he believed to be infected. Plunging his knife deep into one of the suspect cows, he reached into the body to find the lungs and glands full of the disease. He then removed a nodule from an udder, sliced the abnormal growth and held it out for the audience to see a "sickening mixture of milk and pus." He informed his audience, "That is what you've been selling to people for milk."

By 1907, Glover had his veterinary school.

Glover had another concern: the need for mandated inspection of milk and meat. He sought the support of the local citizenry for protective legislation. A prominent local attorney, Paul Lee, helped him draft a pure food ordinance. Mayor Sam Clammer called a meeting of meat and dairy men to discuss the proposed legislation. It took a few meetings and some lively discussion, but ultimately the city adopted pure food ordinances that soon served as models for other cities in Colorado. Under the administration of Theodore Roosevelt, who advocated cleaning up corporate corruption and protecting the rights and safety of consumers, the federal government passed the Pure Food and Drug Act in 1906 and the Meat Inspection Act in 1907. These laws, Glover knew, would call for a notable increase in the number of veterinarians, and he worked tirelessly to bring the new department up to standards set by the U.S. Department of Agriculture; by 1909, the college had a Class A rating.

Businesses received a boost soon after the turn of the century when the chamber of commerce was formed in 1904, with the goal of improving

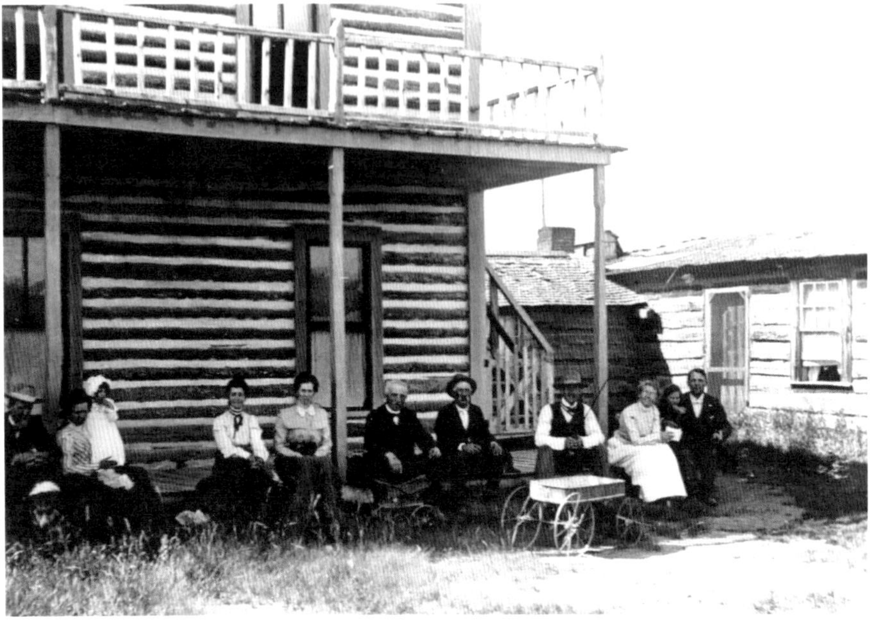

Ansel Watrous is in the center among this group of people enjoying leisure time at a mountain cabin. *H05439.*

streets, enticing tourists and moving toward becoming "a good city." Two hundred people joined, electing A.W. Scott, a druggist, as the first president. The chamber supported the establishment of Rocky Mountain National Park and improving the road up Poudre Canyon, as well as streetlights and street paving, and has remained an active part of the community ever since.

As the population of the town slowly increased, along with a larger student body and broader curricula at the college, the citizens of Fort Collins dealt with changes large and small. The city police department helped maintain law and order; the trolley took passengers all around the town, even as far as the resort at Lindenmeier Lake north of town; automobiles competed with horse-drawn wagons for space on the streets; the dry town attracted a sizable number of churches; the sugar beet factory pumped money into the economy and provided steady jobs; farmers benefitted from research at the college; medical care improved; and the lamb-feeding industry flourished. To those living here at the time, the future must have looked bright indeed.

Chapter 8

In the Early Twentieth Century

Progress

By the second decade of the new century, cars were the clear winners of the transportation competition. On February 26, 1908, photographer H.C. Bradley had invited all the car owners in town to bring their cars to College Avenue for a photo. An auto club had formed in 1907 with the goal of improving roads for car traffic. The image Bradley took, labeled the "auto club" photo, shows thirty-four cars, a large percentage of the fifty or so then traversing the streets of Fort Collins. At the top of the photograph, a Denver and Interurban streetcar lumbers along, pausing long enough for Bradley to get his now legendary shot.

Two years later, the college began a new tradition, College Day, to celebrate college spirit. Students and faculty gathered for a festive picnic on the campus grounds, still centered on the oval. (This event, which evolved into College Days a few decades later, was discontinued in the 1970s after becoming too unruly to be controlled.)

At about this same time, the town was having an annual barbecue, Lamb Day, to celebrate the success of lamb growing in the area. This practice was discontinued a few years later.

The year 1910 saw a link to the past disappear when a major change to the downtown area occurred on January 27: Union Pacific held an auction of structures it had purchased on Jefferson Street, seeking to get them moved or demolished to make way for a railroad station on the north side of the road. More than one hundred buildings went on the auction block, including

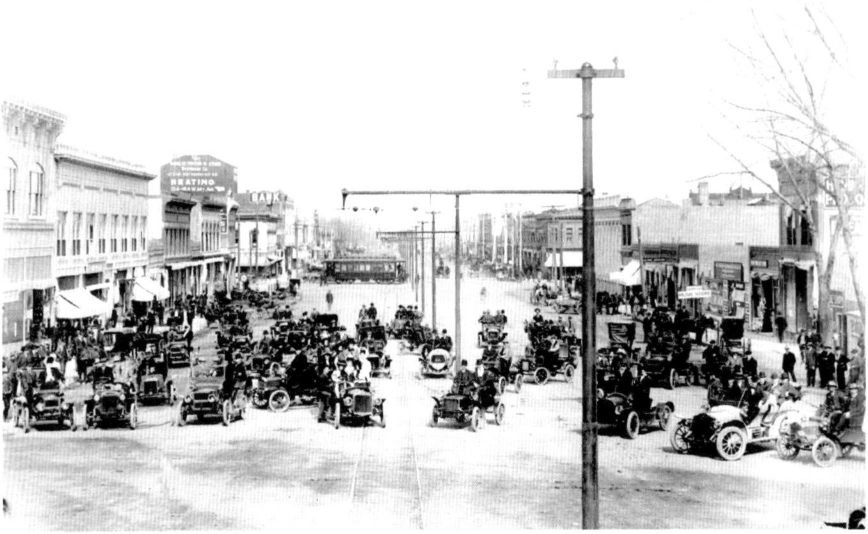

H.C. Bradley took this iconic photograph of almost all the autos in Fort Collins, lined up on College Avenue, in 1908. *H01568_1908.*

the beautiful Tedmon House hotel; Old Grout (at the time a livery stable); the Collins Secondhand Store, which once belonged to William Stover and was the first commercial brick building in town; and some private homes. Most buildings were dismantled; only a few were relocated. Wagons lined up for blocks waiting to carry the logs and other building materials their new owners had bought. "Poor indeed is the man who cannot afford…at least a residence today," commented the *Weekly Courier* newspaper.

Work proceeded on laying the tracks but was stymied in the courts for about a year when John Hoffman, who owned a flour mill near the track's route, raised legal objections. The railroad finally won the day, and the project went forward.

As had happened when the military camp was dismantled decades before, residents of Fort Collins were looking forward, not backward, and saw the disappearance of old buildings as progress. The concept of historic preservation would not be widely accepted until well into the new century.

At the southwest corner of College Avenue and Oak Street, where once soldiers' bodies had reposed, a federal post office was built in 1912—another sign of growth and progress for Fort Collins.

Another railroad had come to town, and automobiles were steadily growing in number, but horses were still around, still used by many, since

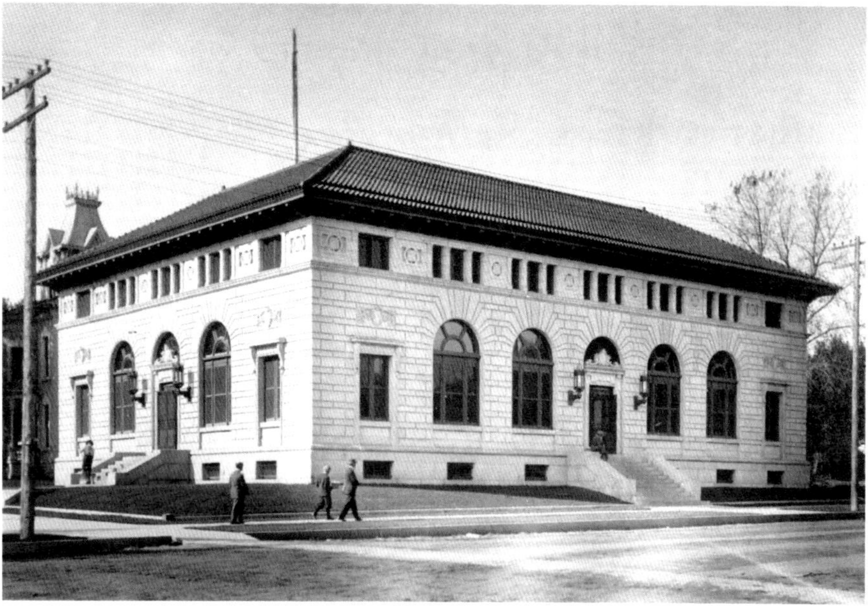

Today an art museum and restaurant, the post office and federal building was constructed in 1911 at the southwest corner of College Avenue and Oak Street. *H07736.*

the gas stations taken for granted nowadays were anything but ubiquitous. Until 1910, car owners purchased gasoline by the barrel and stored it in or near their homes, pouring it into the gas tank one container at a time. A Bowser gas pump arrived in that year at the Hawthorne garage, the first establishment of its kind in town. Automobiles remained the property of the well-to-do, and although tractors had been manufactured by the middle of the next decade, few farmers could afford to buy one, so horses continued to pull hand-held plows.

In December 1913, however, many were grateful that there were still draft horses, for on the first day of that month it began to snow, and snow, and snow, all over the state. By the end of the week, the storm had turned into a blizzard. About three feet of snow fell here, but the big problem was the wind, which whipped the snow around, creating great piles of white stuff everywhere—drifts higher than vehicles or people.

Schools closed. Businesses closed. Farmers struggled to get feed to their livestock. Not even the trolley cars, with their broad metal cattle catchers in front, could get through the drifts. Railroad tracks, buried in snow, were cleared by horse-drawn plows—only the sturdy beasts were powerful enough to get through the drifts. In one instance, sixteen horses

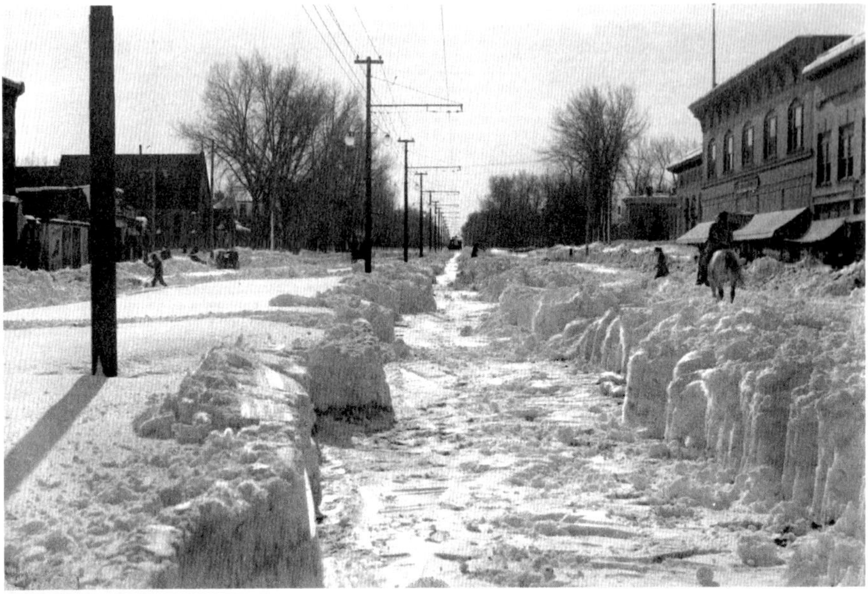

Except for horses, traffic came to a halt on December 1, 1913, when it snowed. The blizzard had an impact on the entire state, not just Fort Collins. *H01217.*

pulled a single plow. No sooner would the tracks be cleared than drifts would bury them again.

Automobile traffic, such as it was, came to a complete standstill. The small, light vehicles were not built to deal with deep snow. Mail could not be delivered (carrier delivery had started in 1901). Most homes were heated with coal that came by train. The coal supply was getting dangerously low before the trains started running regularly again.

For several days, the only system working was the telephone. At the central office, operators heroically stayed on the job night and day keeping communication lines open. So intense and exhausting was the effort that two operators fainted at their desks.

It was a full month before life returned to normal. The Blizzard of 1913 was one for the record books and one in which horses played a part. By that year, an officially recognized police department had been organized, with Albert Baker as the first chief.

A little-known historic event occurred in 1915, when the first transcontinental telephone line, linking one end of the country to the other, came through the Fort Collins exchange. Alexander Graham Bell himself spoke on the line. A few of the original poles can be found even today.

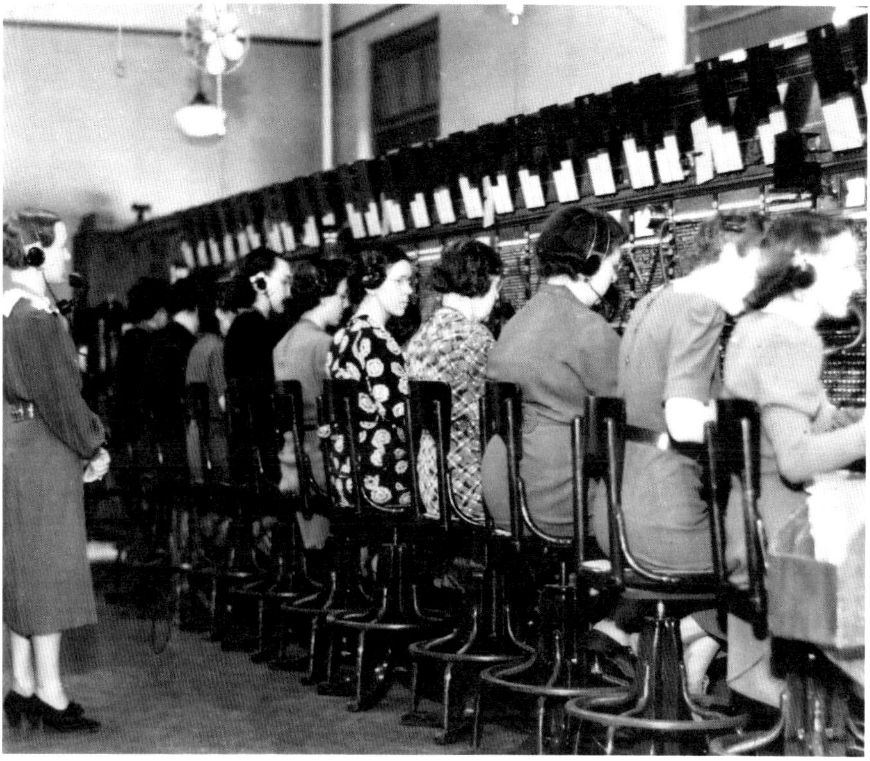

Although this image was taken several years after the blizzard, it illustrates how the telephone exchange operated then, just as it did until 1952, when the change to dial telephones occurred. *H22642.*

Meanwhile, on the broader stage, Europe was at war, and isolationism prevailed in the United States; life went on in the small college town in Colorado much as it had for decades. Yet changes continued to come. Residents were charged with excitement when three blocks of College Avenue were paved, the first street to be done here, in 1916. Streetlights were installed and hitching posts removed; the era of the horse had come to an end. Modernization was moving forward.

Conservationists celebrated the dedication of Rocky Mountain National Park, north and west of Fort Collins, in 1915, as the tenth national park in the country, a designation brought about in large part by the efforts of Enos Mills, who had come west seeking a cure for tuberculosis, stayed to climb Long's Peak and come to treasure the area so much that he dedicated all his efforts toward the creation of the park. Roosevelt National Forest, first called Colorado National Forest, had been set aside in 1910.

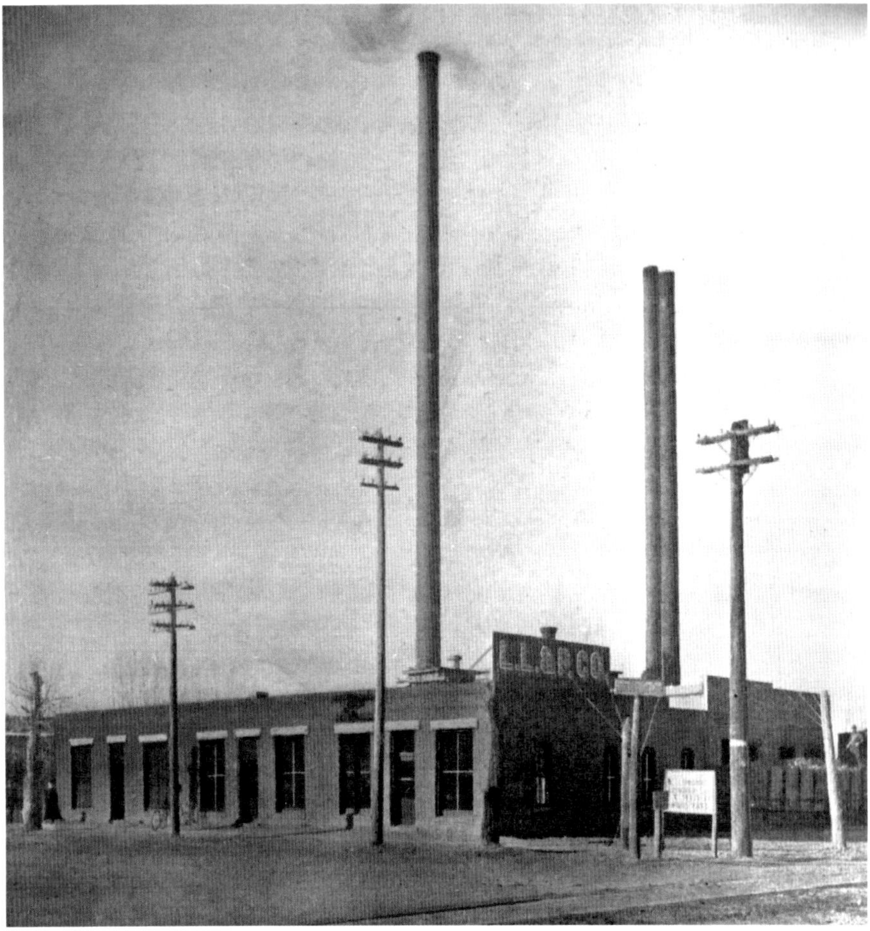

This building was an early power plant on College Avenue, a private company preceding the takeover by municipal power in the 1930s. *H01867.*

At the college, with increasing enrollment and a broader curriculum, President Charles Lory was approaching his second decade as the top administrator, a longer tenure than any of his predecessors. By 1914, enrollment was over five hundred. Under Lory's leadership, more extracurricular activities, including sports, were enhancing students' experiences.

Greek houses had come to the campus early in the new century, welcome because the college did not have dormitories and dining rooms to house and feed the students. "Yet," says Hansen, "the nagging question remained… should 'democracy's college' encourage an institution whose membership connoted exclusivity and arbitrary discrimination against the majority?"

Those who favored fraternities and sororities pointed out that they fostered responsibility and school spirit. The Greek houses soon became integral to campus life, the exclusivity question moot. Lory himself had been a member of a fraternity at the University of Colorado, where he matriculated.

In the spring of 1917, however, many young men were called to serve when the United States was finally drawn into the war in Europe. George Beach, a graduate of Fort Collins High School, was the first soldier from Larimer County killed in the war. More would follow. German immigrants, including the many Germans from Russia who had settled here to work in the sugar beet industry, experienced significant discrimination. Schools dropped the study of German. Some people of German descent changed the spelling of their names; some were refused service at local businesses.

Larimer County sent more than one thousand men to war. On the homefront, citizens raised about $4 million to aid the war effort. Though the war and its consequent devastation of Europe were far away, its impact was felt powerfully here.

But closer to home than the destruction and death the war brought was the influenza epidemic that swept the world in 1918–19. While the worst of the pandemic hit in areas with large, densely housed populations, Fort Collins did not escape. By October 1918, the flu had arrived in nearby Boulder, where a fraternity house became a temporary hospital. Reacting quickly to avoid a widespread epidemic, on October 11, Fort Collins mayor Fred Stover ordered schools, churches, theaters and other public places shut down for the duration, however long that might be.

Soldiers housed at the college fell ill and were cared for in the civil engineering building. Lory ordered tents set up on campus to house the healthy soldiers. The Presbyterian church near campus prepared to take in patients. More temporary hospitals appeared as the epidemic spread. The people of Fort Collins were under a severe quarantine. Soon, physicians began to fall ill.

Patients were advised to take to their beds, eat plenty of nourishing food and stay quiet. They should remain in bed for two or three days even after the fever had abated, use sanitary measures such as not sharing drinking cups or towels and avoid anyone who coughed or sneezed in the vicinity. No doubt trying to avert general panic, officials said that, above all, no one should worry. If they followed these instructions, people were assured, they had a good chance of escaping complications such as bronchitis or pneumonia.

Throughout the winter and into 1919, the flu continued to rage, but here it had decreased enough by March that quarantine measures were lifted and normal business resumed. The low death rate here was due in large part, according to Dr. Henson, to the volunteer efforts of the American Red Cross and the actions of the Larimer County Public Health Association. Red Cross volunteers worked tirelessly at temporary hospitals to aid patients and maintain sanitary conditions. The health association informed, prepared and treated the public.

The epidemic provided impetus nationwide for continued research to find vaccines to prevent such deadly diseases and means to combat bacterial illnesses, for more sanitary conditions in hospitals and for modern hospital facilities. The eventual result in Fort Collins was Larimer County Hospital, soon to replace the private hospitals and the poor farm facility.

More changes, both cultural and economic, were on the horizon for Fort Collins. With the population slowly but steadily increasing, the small high plains town was coming face to face with technological progress along with ways to meet the needs of the increasing population. The breakout of war in Mexico, starting in about 1910, led to the exodus of thousands of citizens, not a few of whom came to Colorado to work in the fields. Fort Collins saw an influx of Mexican immigrants during the decade that the Mexican war lasted. By this time, a large number of the Germans from Russia had moved to better housing than that offered by the sugar beet factory, so the Mexicans lived mainly in the three colonies area (Andersonville, Buckingham and Alta Vista). The immigrants were not easily integrated into the wider community, an issue that would take decades to mitigate.

Yet the small town was steadily growing more cosmopolitan, more in tune with the wider world. The impacts of the War to End All Wars, as it was known then, followed by the flu epidemic, were deeply felt. Though the residents entered the Roaring Twenties with spirit and energy, the town remained dry and relatively staid.

Chapter 9

From War to War

Isolationism

Women had been granted the vote nationwide in 1920. For the first time in the history of the nation, the distaff side had a say in national politics. Fort Collins women had been voting for more than two decades, but this was their first foray onto the national scene. When Franklin Delano Roosevelt, candidate for vice president, came to Fort Collins to give a speech in 1920, many newly enfranchised women were in the audience at the Opera House.

The year 1920 also saw the formal establishment of the Larimer County Public Health Association, headquartered in Fort Collins and financed in the beginning by the sale of Red Cross tuberculosis stamps. The organization's goal was to help people without sufficient resources obtain dental, surgical or other medical care. A visit to the doctor cost $1.50, and a house call cost $3.00—substantial amounts at the time. Measles, whooping cough, typhoid and scarlet fever often surfaced, along with the more common colds and light cases of influenza—the only inoculation available at the time being for smallpox. After the flu, epidemic doctors and patients were much more aware of the havoc diseases can cause. Built in 1925 on land where the poor farm had been, at a cost of $175,000, the new Larimer County Hospital finally offered patients modern facilities and up-to-date care. That year, the hospital served over fourteen thousand patients, one more sign of progress and change.

Women's gaining the vote was the first of many changes to happen both nationally and locally. Thanks to Henry Ford's decision to manufacture a car

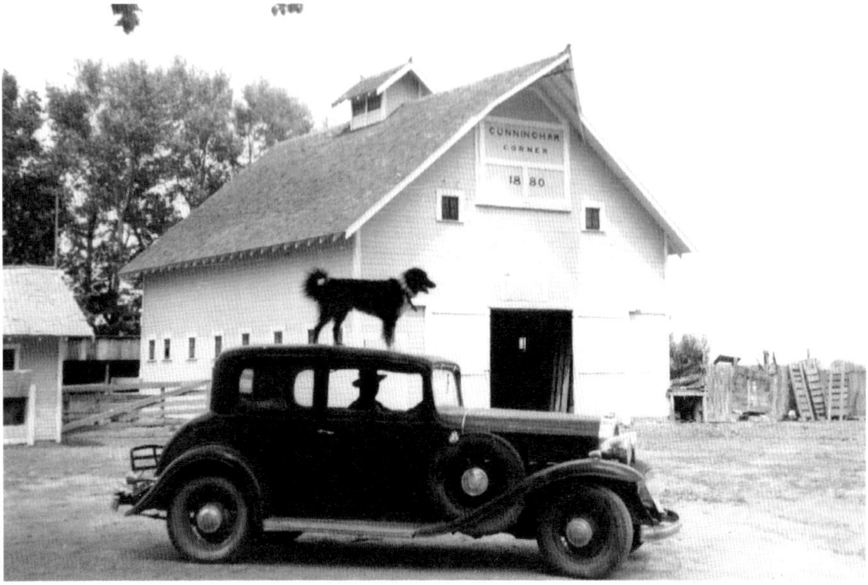

For decades, the barn at the northeast corner of Horsetooth Road and Shields Street stood as a local landmark, Cunningham Corner, now replaced by Cunningham Corner Villas. The barn was preserved and moved to private land. *Courtesy of Danny Rogers.*

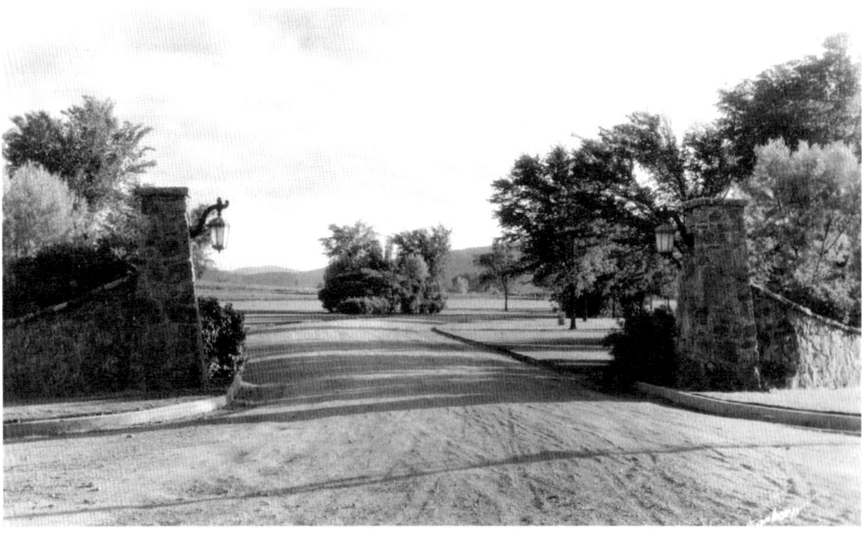

City Park, a popular camping spot for motorists in the 1920s and '30s, welcomed visitors at this attractive entrance. *H09074.*

his employees could afford, the average individual could now buy one; more and more automobiles were appearing on the roads. As a consequence, roads were being paved and widened and gas stations with pumps were cropping up all over the country, including here. Touring in autos became quite popular.

City Park opened the grounds for use by tourists and visitors from out of town as an overnight camping spot. The camp was so well used that local hotel owners became concerned about their profits. Despite that anxiety, a new hotel, the Armstrong, was constructed at the northwest corner of Olive Street and College Avenue in 1923 and flourished thanks to the main road that ran through town—what is now U.S. Highway 287. The Armstrong is, as of this writing, the only hotel in downtown Fort Collins.

In that same year, oil was discovered north of Wellington, a small town north of Fort Collins. Union Oil opened the Mitchell Well in 1924. The oil-rich area stretched for miles and brought the curious in droves; one day, thousands of people lined up to see the well (something that would never be allowed today, with environmental protections in place). Fortunately, no visitors were nearby on July 23, 1924, when an electrical spark caused a spectacular fire that could be seen for miles and which took twenty-four days to extinguish. Spectators did come, but kept at a safe distance. Perhaps the fire was a forerunner of doom, for despite the optimism that pervaded the town when oil was struck, with the newspaper predicting a population of fifty thousand people and prosperity for all, the oil industry had fizzled out by the 1930s, nearly forgotten.

Charles Boettcher, who had in the previous century owned a small hardware store north of town, had become a very wealthy man. In 1927, he opened the Ideal Cement Company near Laporte, an industry that brought with it welcome employment and churned out cement for many decades, changing hands and names on occasion, until finally closing for good in 2005. By the time it closed, many employees were second- or third-generation workers.

With a population close to ten thousand, residents concluded that a new high school was in order. Land was secured south of town, and the sturdy brick structure was open for students in 1925 at 1400 Remington Street. Some complained that it was too far out of town, but students managed to get there, on foot or on the trolley (the lumbering Interurban cars had been replaced in 1919 with smaller Birney cars on a municipal line), which dropped them off on Pitkin Street. The school featured a gymnasium, thus encouraging a sports program (girls could play sports but did not compete),

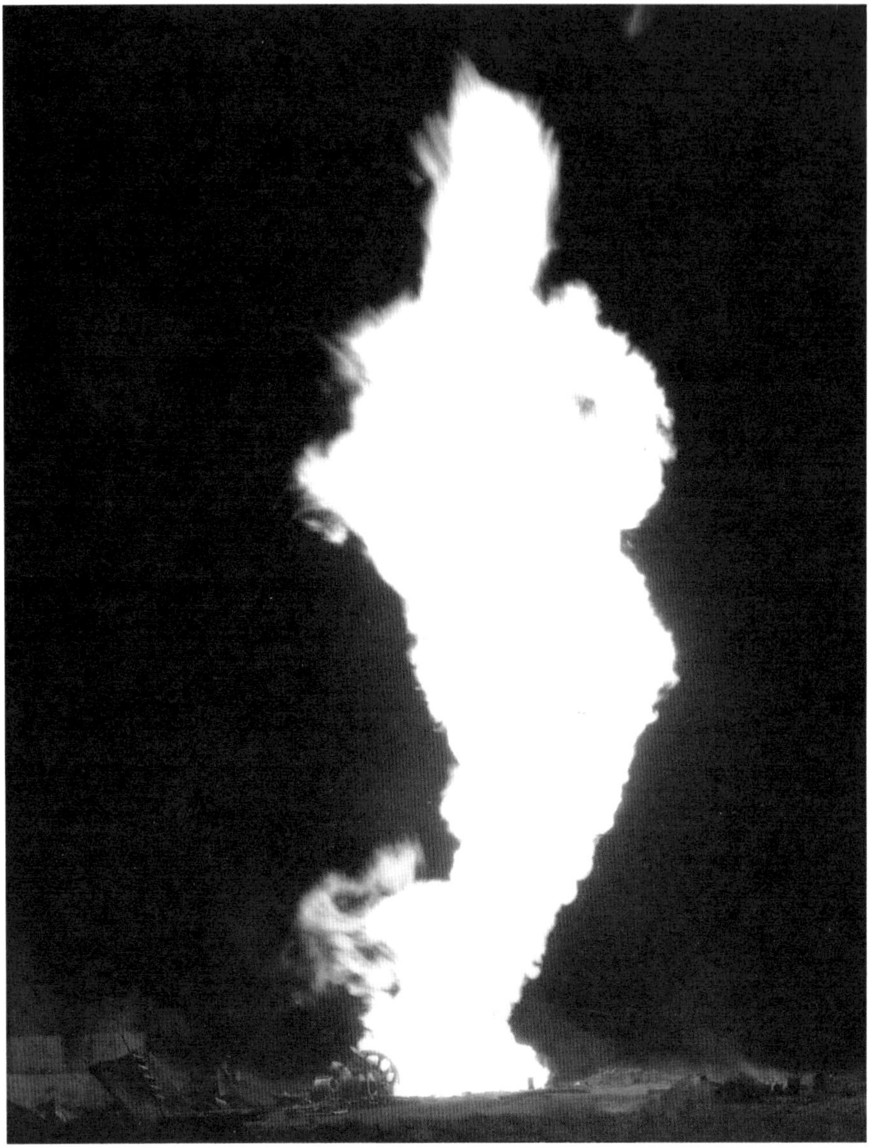

Against the darkened sky, flames from the fire at the Mitchell oil well near Wellington shot upward in July 1924. Unprotected spectators came to watch. *H09110.*

and in 1927, the track team won permanent possession of a track trophy for winning three times at the national level. Because of the thriving sheep-feeding industry in the area, a lambkin was chosen as the school mascot, still the same today although the high school moved to a new building in 1995.

After the move, the university acquired the building, added an auditorium and turned it into a center for the arts.

In the aftermath of the Great War, American society adopted a carefree, hedonistic posture, paying little heed to the outside world. America became radically isolationist and patriotic in reaction to the horrendous toll the war had taken. The Ku Klux Klan's message of patriotic fervor and nationalism fit right in with the current mood in Colorado and nationwide.

Thus, it was not difficult for the KKK to infiltrate the politically dominant Republican Party in Colorado.

This was not the Klan's first venture into our state. History records some isolated incidents in the 1880s, the targets being African Americans, Catholics, Jews and Hispanics. Because few African Americans lived in our state at that time, the KKK turned their attentions elsewhere and sometimes drove people from their homes. However, it was not until the 1920s that the Klan's actions in Colorado received much attention. The Klan became officially incorporated as an organization in the state with a goal of "purifying" the state by occupying the majority of public offices, local and statewide. By the mid-1920s, it had successfully elected a governor, lieutenant governor, secretary of state and mayor of Denver. Before long, membership throughout the state was more than thirty thousand.

As it had in other Colorado communities, the Klan arrived in Fort Collins and was accepted as a legitimate organization. Drawn in by the patriotic rhetoric, Samuel Salyers, who owned a small grocery store, joined and was elected exalted Cyclops of the Fort Collins klavern in 1924. Soon afterward, white-robed, hooded Klansmen marched in the streets of our town and rallied on a hill in City Park. There, Salyers finally discovered the depths of the Klan's profound hatred of Catholics, Jews and others. Deeply dismayed and feeling deceived, Salyers denounced the klavern's prejudicial beliefs. As a Christian, he maintained they should have charity toward all.

The klavern summarily dismissed Salyers. Members of the klavern were told to boycott his grocery store; others would not shop there for fear of retaliation even though they did not belong to the Klan. Salyers faced ruin, but he stood his ground.

We do not know what happened to him subsequently; his grocery store disappears from the city directory a few years after this dramatic confrontation. However, his story received attention throughout Colorado; not long after what happened here, a statewide bipartisan group began investigating the Klan, ultimately forcing it out of the Republican Party. By 1926, the Klan's influence had diminished considerably.

The prosperity, isolationism and gaiety that had settled into the American psyche came to an abrupt and shocking end in October 1929, when the stock market crashed. Fort Collins was hit as hard as anywhere else. Farmers and merchants went bankrupt, and banks shut down; people were frightened and depressed.

Unemployment in Larimer County crept up to about 35 percent within a short time. A drought did not help matters; in town, the council imposed severe restrictions on lawn watering, and the Poudre River was at its lowest since the 1860s. High school graduates of the time recalled one dust storm so severe that they could not see three feet in front of them. Grasshoppers and the Mormon cricket further plagued hard-pressed farmers. The agricultural experiment station at the college worked tirelessly to alleviate these problems.

Amidst the troubles and challenges that pervaded here, a new industry came to be. In 1931, J.D. Forney, who had once gotten a ticket for driving too fast around the oval while courting his wife-to-be, invented a new kind of soldering iron that greatly aided farmers with their machinery. Although he sometimes took payment in kind during the Depression, Forney's device was successful enough that he built a factory on West Laporte Avenue. Years later, in 1949, the factory caught fire. Because it was outside the city limits, the fire department couldn't fight it, but it left the hoses. Forney Industries is still in operation, still on West Laporte Avenue.

In time, Forney grew wealthy enough to indulge his love of antique cars. He collected so many that he opened a museum, which eventually outgrew the space and relocated to Denver, where it houses not only antique cars but also trains and bicycles.

Amidst the depths of the Depression, city managers decided that the coffers needed more revenue. One way to do that, they concluded, was to provide municipal electricity. Up to that point, electricity had been delivered by private owners, who could charge whatever they wanted. Accordingly, the city set about to acquire rights and build a power plant. The Public Service Company of Colorado, which had been providing power, resisted this move, and the dispute ended up in court. Ultimately, the city won, and a new power plant was up and running by 1935, bringing in the steady revenue stream the city's budget needed. The plant, located on the north side of the river and the east side of College Avenue, now belongs to the university, serving as an energy and conversion facility.

Another bright light during the dark times was the triumph of CAC graduate Glenn Morris, who went to Berlin in 1936 to compete in the Olympics and won the decathlon. Morris went on to a star-crossed career, playing football, playing Tarzan in films and bringing glory to his alma mater, although his career did not last, and he died in obscurity. The old field house on the campus, which faces onto South College Avenue, bears his name.

Three factors helped Fort Collins survive the Great Depression with less impact than many places experienced: the agricultural college (renamed Colorado Agricultural and Mechanical College in 1935) continued to function, providing employment and a flow of money into the town; the sugar beet factory kept on producing sugar, employing field and factory workers; and the college's Extension Service reached out to the rural community to help women learn more effective ways of preparing and preserving food and to help farmers improve their yields and conserve water during the drought. Franklin Roosevelt's Civilian Conservation Corps (CCC) also aided the economy when military-style camps were set up in nearby Poudre Canyon and in Big Thompson Canyon to build roads, including Trail Ridge Road in Rocky Mountain National Park; forge hiking trails; and create mountain parks. The men who worked in these military-style camps all over the country

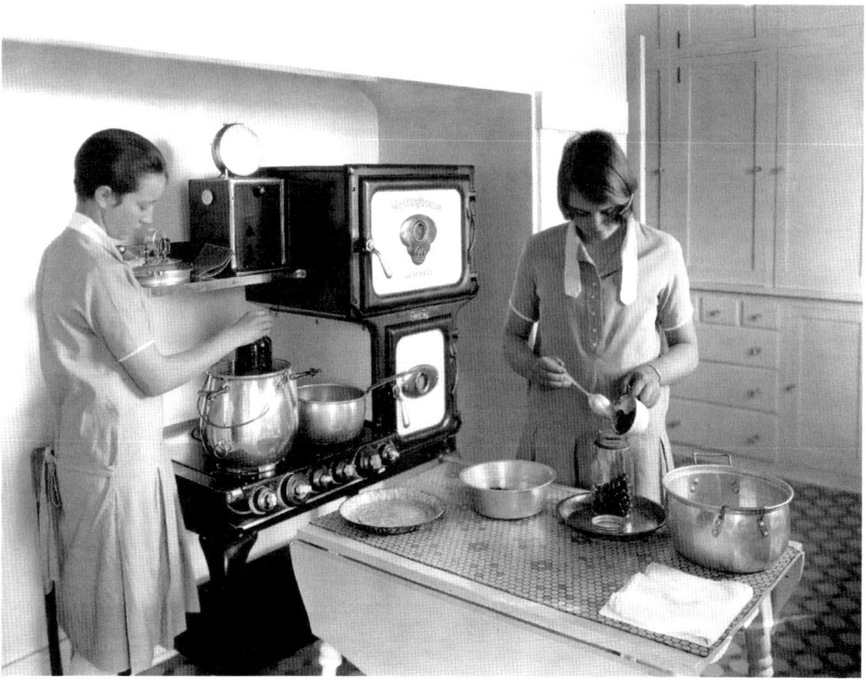

During the Great Depression, the Agricultural Extension Service provided invaluable aid to homemakers; here, agents work in a test kitchen on canning procedures. *H07736.*

went on to become the core of the armed forces, which fought so well when World War II broke out.

For the majority of residents, life went on as usual during the Depression. No one had much money, but people were resourceful and cooperative. A Cunningham descendant, Fanny, wrote about a 1930s excursion up Poudre Canyon, near Chambers Lake, to clear the Michigan Ditch, during which workers encountered snow so deep they were stranded for several days. Hardened by adversity, they endured the situation gamely and emerged in good spirits.

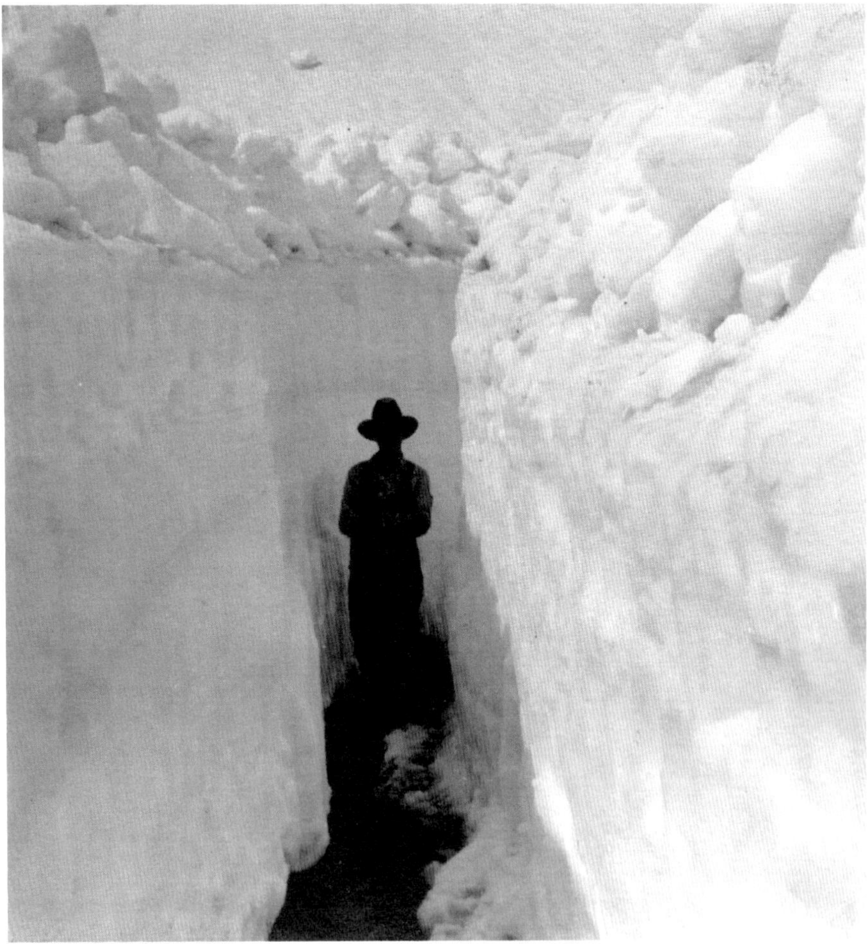

Every spring, workers made their way up to Poudre Canyon to clear the Michigan Ditch before the snowmelt began. Some years, like this one, the snow could be quite deep. *Courtesy of Danny Rogers.*

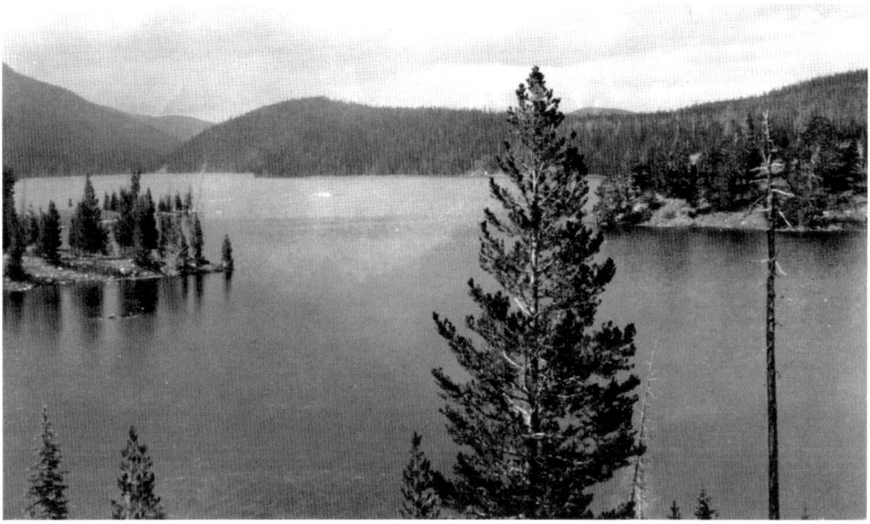

Chambers Lake, a natural lake near the top of Poudre Canyon where a murder once took place, is today a favorite camping spot. *Courtesy of Danny Rogers.*

On a January day in 1939, long before Occupational Safety and Health Administration (OSHA) regulations were enacted, the late local historian Arlene Ahlbrandt was in grade school in Wellington when the building shook and the sound of an explosion was so enormous that she "thought the world was coming to an end." In Laporte, nearer to the blast site, glass was flying, car windows were shattering and debris was everywhere. A large crater created by the blast broke a water main.

The explosion had happened at the Ideal Cement plant, where workers had been thawing some dynamite intended for use in a quarry. Somehow the stuff ignited and blew, demolishing the garage where the workers had put the dynamite, as well as three truckloads of explosives parked outside the garage. One wall of the plant itself was blown out. Relatives frantically tried to learn about survivors at the plant, and for many, the news was terrible. Several men were killed and others severely injured.

The tragedy on the homefront would pale next to what the world was about to get embroiled in, but residents did not know what lay ahead when it happened. The city mourned and carried on.

By the next year, 1940, Fort Collins had six elementary schools, several of which had been designed by Montezuma Fuller, as well as Lincoln Junior High School (the former high school) and Fort Collins High School. And at the college, after serving longer than any other president in the college's history, Charles Lory retired. Lory had broadened the curriculum, seen the college through the Depression, hired outstanding faculty (see Hansen for specifics) and helped the college achieve "a vital equilibrium—a healthy balance between resident instruction, research, and extension service" thanks to his wise and "skillful" administration. The grassy green, fondly called "the oval," aka "lover's lane," which was the center of the campus for many years was developed under Lory's leadership. Today, Lory State Park west of Horsetooth Reservoir and Lory Student Center on the campus honor his time at the college.

However, the world was poised to intrude on the small, stable, rather insular community. On December 7, 1941, the "day of infamy," the Japanese bombed Pearl Harbor, and everything changed once more. Fort Collins's first casualty was Ben Schlecht, formerly a student at FCHS, who was killed at Pearl Harbor. Very soon afterward, Fort Collins had another local war hero. Bert Christman, born here in 1915, went to New York City to become an artist, drew the "Scorchy Smith" comic strip about a heroic aviator for a time and then became fascinated with flying and took lessons. In 1940, he joined Claire Chennault's volunteer Flying Tigers in air raids intended to keep the Burma Road open. He was shot down while bailing out of a plane in January 1942. An airfield on West Laporte Avenue was named for him.

Along with the rest of the country, Fort Collins citizens pitched in wholeheartedly for the war effort. Children collected tin cans and newspapers, homemakers struggled with rationing, auto repair shops stayed busy keeping cars on the road since no new ones were coming from Detroit and young men went off to war. A civilian defense corps had been empowered even before war began, and from time to time, blackouts and air raid drills were held.

At the college, many teaching positions were taken by women after male professors had joined up. The movie theaters, the Lyric on East Mountain and the America on College Avenue, were crowded with people who wanted to see the latest war happenings as narrated by Movietone News. Radios brought the news into homes, along with the avuncular voice of President Franklin Roosevelt holding his fireside chats. Several women served in various capacities, among them Martha Trimble, the first woman in Larimer County to join the WAVES. She taught navigation to aviation students, returning after the war to a long career teaching English at the college. The family of Courtlyn Hotchkiss, a pilot, had been told that he was dead, and he had in fact been shot down, but he had survived for six months with the help of French citizens and had arrived in Paris not long after the U.S. Army's triumphant march into the city. Encountering an officer who was able to help him, he made his way to the French coast and from there to England, whereupon his family learned that he was alive and well. While there were thousands of stories like his, not all of them had happy endings.

In March 1945, the war came close to home when a balloon carrying incendiary devices landed in a field on the Swets farm in Timnath, exploding but causing no deaths. It developed that the Japanese had launched almost ten thousand of these balloons at the United States in hopes of starting forest fires and explosions to damage morale, a tactic that failed because the media cooperated with the government by not making the incidents public.

With the end of the war in 1945 came a population boom that was destined to continue for decades and is still going on. Thanks to the GI Bill, soldiers came to the college in considerable numbers; many decided to settle here. The small college town so familiar to longtime residents would never be the same again.

Chapter 10

After the War

Discovered

Veterans coming to the college after the war, using the GI Bill to pay their tuitions, were housed in Veterans Village in Quonset huts arrayed along the south side of West Laurel Street because the college had insufficient housing, and many of the veterans were married, so dormitories would not be suitable. The small metal structures, which had served as portable units during wartime and were available by the thousands when the war ended, became homes to veterans for several years after the war. Given what they had been through, Hansen comments, they did not complain about the structures, even though they were hot in summer and terrifying in windstorms.

With the rest of the country, Fort Collins struggled through a midwinter coal strike in 1948. Without coal, schools were forced to close; homeowners had to use small electric or propane heaters, which carried their own dangers; and businesses had to cut hours. After the strike ended and the coal trains moved again, many home and business furnaces were converted to natural gas.

Residents were grateful for a steady supply of heating fuel when nature again reminded the city of its power in January 1949—one of the worst blizzards in the city's history stranded travelers; caused deaths, both humans and livestock; and brought the state to a standstill for days. Hundreds of people could not be reached; after the thaw, some were found frozen. In one instance, a woman went from her house to the mailbox and could not find her way home again. She froze to death in front of her own home.

In time winter abated, and the population continued to grow. Within a little over a decade, the population of Fort Collins had more than doubled, thanks in large part to the influx of veterans.

In response to the need for more water thanks to exponential growth, the city cooperated with other municipalities to create a reservoir where the quarry and the town of Stout had once been. The Colorado–Big Thompson Water Project, begun before World War II and completed by 1958, created Horsetooth Reservoir west of town to supply water to towns in Northern Colorado, including Fort Collins. The area, adjacent to Lory State Park to the west, has become a popular recreation and fishing place, as well as the site of some private homes.

The aftermath of the war brought about the start of a culture shift that had been a long time in coming. Ever since their arrival decades earlier, the Hispanics who worked the beet fields and the factory and mostly lived in adobe houses confined to the three colonies had been discriminated against by local merchants, more than a few of whom posted White Trade Only signs in their windows. Reacting to the discrimination, most Hispanics kept to themselves, some of them choosing not to learn English.

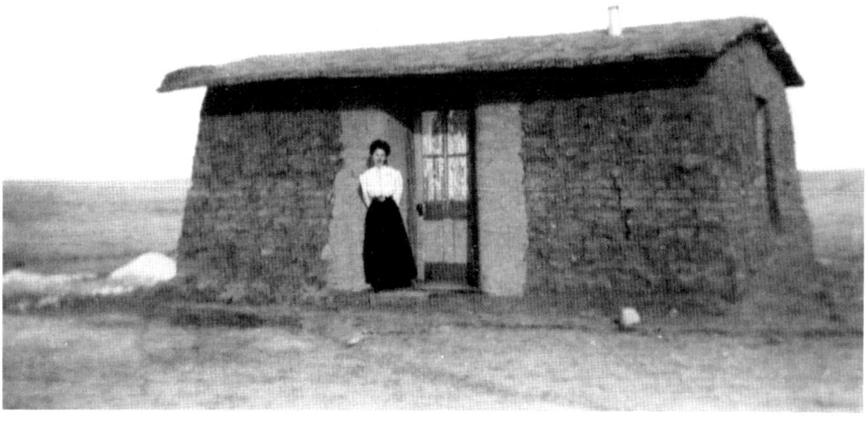

This small adobe home somewhere in Larimer County is typical of those built by immigrants from Mexico in the three colonies. The woman is unidentified. *H10090.*

A Spanish baseball league developed in the 1930s, the teams playing on pothole-filled fields with makeshift balls and gloves; more than a few young people completed only the required schooling. The majority of Hispanics living beyond the three colonies coalesced in a residential area west of College Avenue and north of Laporte Avenue.

One activist Hispanic, Librado "Lee" Martinez, was a powerful voice on the Human Rights Commission. Martinez fought in World War I and lost a son in World War II. An American Legion Post and a city park on land once trod by soldiers are named for him.

A noticeable number of returning veterans were sensitive to this discrimination and protested against it, and a small group of dedicated people, led by Maurice Albertson, worked to have the signs removed, succeeding at last by about 1948. Many Hispanics continued to live in the colonies. Gradually, the town has come to appreciate rather than disparage diversity; today, the city's Human Rights Commission works to ensure fair treatment for all.

With the emergence of the Cold War era in the 1950s, when fear of the spread of communism pervaded, college professors were required to sign loyalty oaths. Some faculty resigned rather than do so.

But as it had done throughout the twentieth century, technology advanced, and Fort Collins, like other towns across the nation, absorbed its impact. Deeply felt here by many longtime residents was the demise of the trolley line.

The little trolleys, known affectionately as "galloping geese" because of their up-and-down motion, lost out to the automobile in 1951. Fort Collins was the last small town in America to have a trolley line; all over the country, cars had won the day. One Birney car, restored years later, now lopes along Mountain Avenue to City Park in the summer for tourists. Bus routes were started, and what was once a railroad station on North Mason Street became the transportation center for the city bus system.

Once having a stronghold on the city's business district, downtown merchants saw commerce slide southward, with a variety of enterprises gradually replacing the stately homes that formerly graced College Avenue. A Safeway store built at the northwest corner of College Avenue and Mulberry Street was one of the first businesses established south of the small downtown enclave.

And as business grew, so did the college, expanding at last beyond the oval, which had been the center of the campus for so many years (with the exception of Old Main, the Industrial Arts Building constructed in the 1880s and a few other buildings). In 1952, college president William Morgan proposed changing the name of the college from Colorado Agricultural and Mechanical

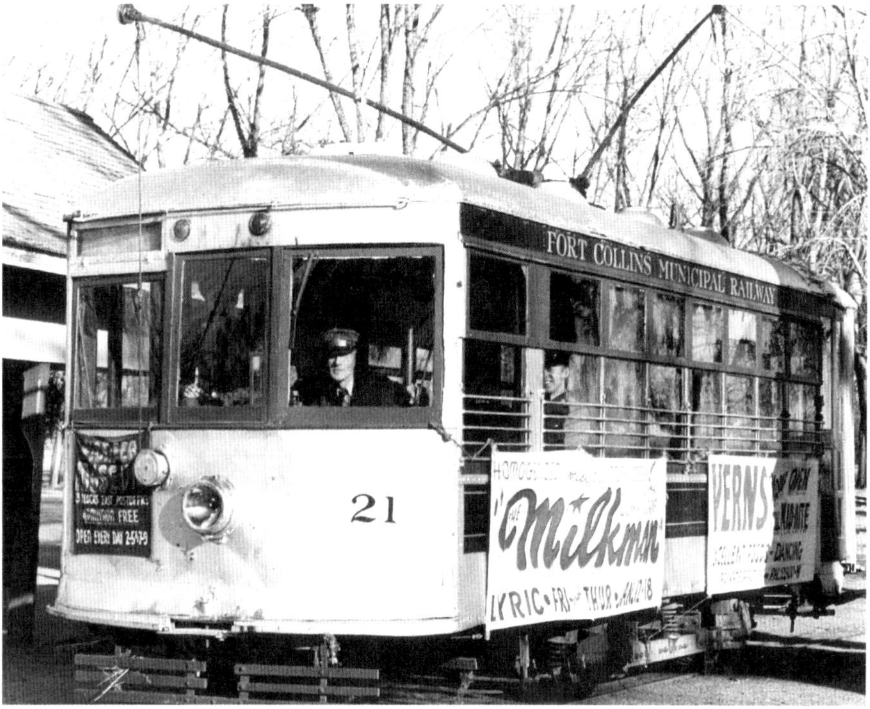

Until the 1950s, when service was discontinued, conductors drove Birney trolley cars, known to townspeople as "galloping geese." *Courtesy of Malcolm McNeill.*

College (A&M) to Colorado State University (CSU) because the school now encompassed far more than technological and scientific courses of study, and the focus had moved away from agriculture. The name change became official in 1957 as the institution grew in enrollment and faculty. The land that had once been a plowed and planted field was being converted to space to hold classroom buildings and dormitories to house the increasing numbers of students.

Sports continued to flourish on the campus. The football team benefitted from the returning veterans. One veteran, Eddie Hanna, has a poignant story. One of the first African Americans to play football at the college, he was a fast and popular running back. In 1949, he scored a winning touchdown in a game against Colorado College and died of a heart attack on the train home. Hanna was only twenty-four.

Along with the expansion of the college to a university, city government also underwent a change—to a council/city manager form of government, which grants the manager powers a mayor formerly had but leaves him or her answerable to the council. The council then chose a mayor each year for a one-year term. The new charter took effect in 1955. (Today, the mayor is elected by the populace at large.) A new city hall, replacing the original one on Walnut Street, was built on Laporte Avenue in 1958 and is still in use, although the police station and jail it originally housed have been relocated to a new station built after the turn of the twenty-first century.

Following the election of John F. Kennedy, two employees of Colorado State University, Pauline Birky Kreutzer and Maurice Albertson, were instrumental in the design and development of the Peace Corps.

As long as anyone could remember at the time, the road from Fort Collins to Denver was U.S. Highway 287, which snaked through Loveland, Berthoud and other towns on its way to the capital. Soon after his administration began, President Dwight Eisenhower initiated the interstate highway system, which by the end of the 1960s connected the state from one end to the other, north–south and east–west, on divided highways that, on the Front Range, went in a smooth, straight line. This enterprise brought Fort Collins in closer touch with the rest of the eastern slope cities and towns and, it is probable, resulted in more growth. By the early 1970s, subdivisions were appearing far beyond the boundaries of the original settlement, mostly to the south, and businesses stretched several miles southward along College Avenue. Foothills Fashion Mall, built around that time, contributed to drawing even more business southward.

Perhaps symbolic of the town's evolution away from the core of agriculture, Great Western Sugar Company closed its doors in 1955. That same year saw a bad flood in August, causing considerable damage to the college campus. For a few days, the oval became a lake.

With about twenty-five thousand inhabitants by the 1950s, it was time for a newer courthouse. As was the case again several decades later, the same site as the original building was selected, and a building costing about $1 million was constructed to replace the aging one. Since then, a third courthouse has been built in the same location, with the earlier one demolished due to asbestos contamination.

The arrival in 1955 of Woodward Governor, a machine tool company, signaled a time of more growth and prosperity. The company brought welcome jobs. First located downtown, Woodward soon built a plant at the northwest corner of Drake Road and Lemay Avenue (the former Hospital Road) and in 2014 broke ground on new headquarters in the downtown area.

As the town evolved into a city and grew more cosmopolitan, a movement to legalize liquor—after seven decades as a dry town—gained momentum, finally succeeding by majority vote in 1969. This began to alter the character of the town, especially downtown, where taverns appeared and restaurants could serve wine and other libations. Before prohibition ended here, residents could buy liquor just outside of town, including at a restaurant on North College called the Covered Wagon and at a nightclub east of town called the Safari. Bootlegging was known to the police, although perpetrators were seldom caught—but by the first decades of the twentieth century, druggists no longer sold alcoholic medicinal concoctions as regulation of drugs took hold.

At the height of the Cold War, in 1961, an intercontinental ballistic missile made its very public way through Fort Collins. It was installed in a launch site northwest of Fort Collins, placing the high plains community right in the middle of a potential nuclear war. Today, records are stored in the long-abandoned silo.

On June 28, 1965, an anonymous caller informed the fire department of a blaze at the State Dry Goods Company, a department store that had been at the northwest corner of College Avenue and Oak Street for many years. Dentists and other professionals had offices above the store. Fortunately, the fire began late at night, so no one was in the building; therefore, the firefighters reasoned, no one would get hurt or die.

Using much better tools than volunteers had had at their disposal when the Welch Block caught fire and two people died, the firemen got to work. Then suddenly, with no warning, the south wall collapsed, landing on fire chief Cliff Carpenter, who was directing operations from the sidewalk, and fireman James Wichtel before they could get out of the way. Digging frantically, the firemen found their chief dead and Wichtel badly injured. The store suffered damage in the millions and did not reopen. Wichtel survived, and Fort Collins mourned a tragic loss.

Though rumors spread that the fire might have been started by teenage boys playing with firecrackers, fire department records show that it was in fact caused by faulty wiring in the basement.

The city also felt the impact of the restless late 1960s and early '70s. Demonstrations were held here; protestors marched in favor of the Equal Rights Amendment and against the war in Vietnam. A large number of students on campus were involved in the struggle for civil rights in the South, forming a Black Student Alliance and a Mexican American Committee for Equality and, for a brief time, occupying the administration building.

For the most part, the protests were nonviolent, with one visible and tragic exception. On May 8, 1970, Old Main burned to the ground. Luckily, the fire happened at night when no one was in the building, but many professors who had offices there lost all of their books and papers. The auditorium, long used as a performance hall; the classrooms with their high windows; the old, wooden floors that creaked—all gone. Though no perpetrator was ever caught, it was believed that the fire had been set in some kind of pointless protest, a symptom of the times.

Another fire in 1975 killed a man at the Northern Hotel, then being used mainly by those who could not afford to live anywhere else. Today, the restored Northern houses senior citizens, with businesses on the ground floor.

A different kind of disaster struck in 1977, when the Elks building on Remington Street, which had been designed by Montezuma Fuller and built in 1904 as a YMCA, exploded. More than one hundred downtown businesses were damaged by the explosion, which was probably caused by a leaky gas valve; the sound was heard for miles around. Debris was thrown as far as four blocks away, and windows were shattered. The Elks rebuilt and occupied the building until selling it in the 2000s in expectation of a downtown hotel being built on the site.

After a series of articles in the local newspaper detailing living conditions in the three colonies, sewer systems were installed, and the streets were paved in the 1970s.

In that same time period, a new interest in historic preservation emerged, though not before several notable buildings, including downtown churches, had been razed. Avery House, once the gracious home of Franklin and his family, became a local landmark preserved and managed by the Poudre Landmarks Foundation. Restoration on the old waterworks on Overland Trail began. Amid some controversy, the impetus for historic preservation resulted in the restoration of a Birney trolley car for summer tourists to ride, with the tracks going along Mountain Avenue from College Avenue to City Park. The old car had sat in Library Park, deteriorating, for years before the Municipal Railway Association undertook to bring it back to life.

Downtown Fort Collins, which had also been allowed to deteriorate for some years, was revitalized to become a lively, active center of dining and commerce. The Downtown Development Association (DDA) completed an upgrade of College Avenue in 1978, and more changes and upgrades have come since then. Building façades have been preserved even though the purposes of the establishments within have changed. When Disneyland was built, Walt Disney used downtown Fort Collins and his hometown in Missouri as models for the design of Main Street, thanks to the childhood memories of artist Harper Goff, who had lived here many years earlier.

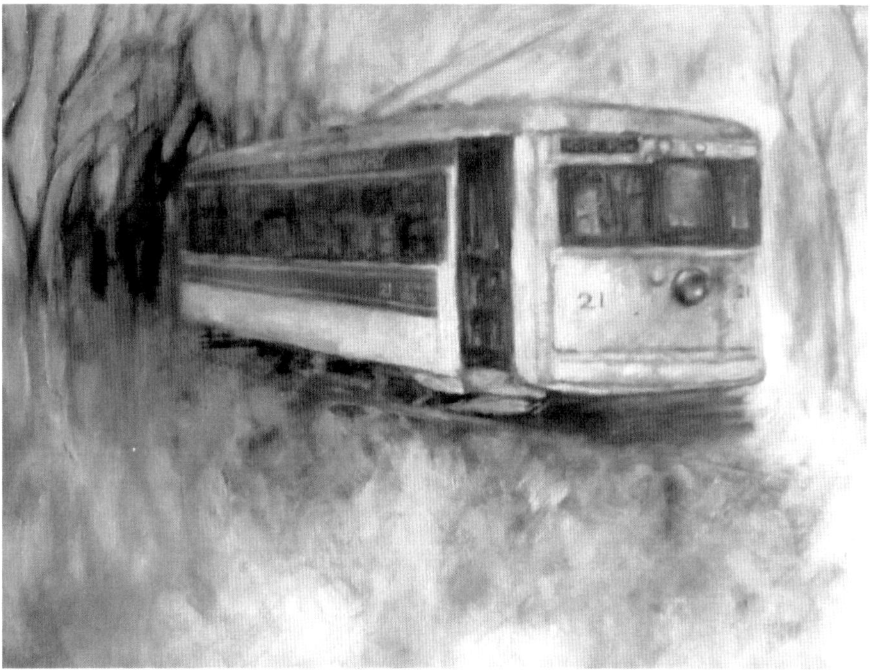

Birney car number 21 sat neglected in Library Park from the 1950s until restoration began decades later. *Painting by and courtesy of Frances E. Lane, photographed by Patrick Clements.*

In 1985 Thomas Sutherland, a CSU professor who was teaching at American University in Beirut, Lebanon, was taken hostage. He and cellmate Terry Anderson, a widely known journalist, were held captive for six and a half years. While Sutherland was held hostage, yellow ribbons ringed tree trunks all over town; when he was released, a joyous celebration was held at the college gymnasium.

Water treatment entered a new phase in 1987, when the old plant in Poudre Canyon was shut down, fully replaced by the present plant on West Laporte Avenue, which had been constructed in 1969 with some subsequent expansions.

Perhaps the most memorable event that occurred before the new millennium was a flash flood in July 1997 that killed six people who lived in a low-lying mobile home park on College Avenue and caused widespread damage. Spring Creek, normally a placid, slow-flowing body of water, overflowed that night and brought devastation in its wake. In response to the unexpected and tragic event, the city put in a new, larger drainage system in hopes of preventing a repeat of that tragedy.

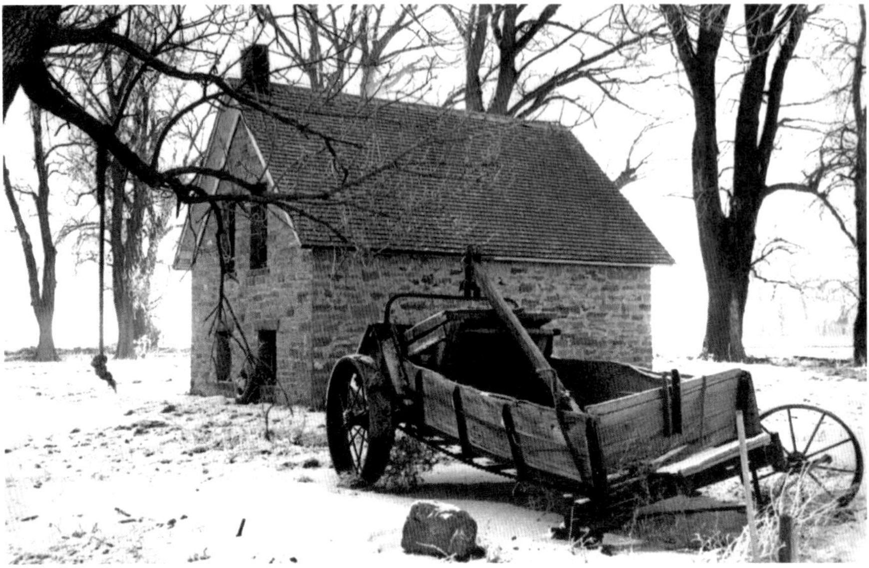

All that remains of John Nelson's once prosperous dairy farm is the milk house, which is symbolic of the preservation efforts that began in the 1970s. *H11710.*

Honoring the legacy of hardworking Hispanics who built adobe homes in the three colonies, a fine example of a typical adobe home was preserved and restored to become a small museum of Hispanic life and culture, the Museo de las Tres Colonias. Once the Romero home, one of many such houses erected by Hispanics in Buckingham and Andersonville during the beet factory years, the house typically had no indoor plumbing and only a cold room for refrigeration. John Romero built the home adobe brick by adobe brick, and the Romeros raised a large family there, as had many other Hispanic families in homes like that one.

Today, aid and resources that were not on hand for such families then are available for all who need assistance.

Even though the growing city continues to inch out, mostly south and east, with new subdivisions and shopping centers, businesses and commerce; even though the campus stretches far beyond the school's original location; even though changes tumble upon changes, the town that began here two centuries ago lives on in those who preserve and record its history, a history that tells tales of courage, persistence, innovation, struggle, setbacks, triumphs and more. They are the stories of the people who lived here and laid a foundation that has grown into a city far beyond anything they ever envisioned.

Epilogue

Through the Founders' Eyes

In 1914, upon the fiftieth anniversary of the founding of Fort Collins, F.C. Grable, a local farmer, rhapsodized about the future of the place he had chosen for his home. "Were I asked where in the whole world was to be found the most beautiful and productive agricultural area, I would unhesitatingly answer—the Cache la Poudre Valley." He went on to refer to the abundance of crops that would continue to grow happily here. He concluded, "Land, bountiful land. The king on his throne lives in poverty of riches compared to the king of the soil on his little farm in the far famed valley of the Cache la Poudre."

Like most of his compatriots, Grable envisioned a future centered on agriculture. How astounded they would be to find a thriving community of over 150,000 people; a campus that extends west and south far beyond the oval around which the college began, with over 30,000 students; an abundance of traffic lights; the trains an impediment instead of an essential means of transporting people and goods.

Fort Collins has left its farming and ranching roots far behind, consigned to the mists of history. The dairy herd begun in 1883 was sold off in 1989; residents of the houses surrounding it were unhappy with the noise and odors—a further symptom of urbanization.

Today, the settlement laid out so carefully by Franklin Avery has been swallowed by houses and businesses in every direction—yet Avery could still find the town he platted, albeit changed. Where farms once produced crops, houses now crop up. Instead of wide, dusty streets adorned with horse dung,

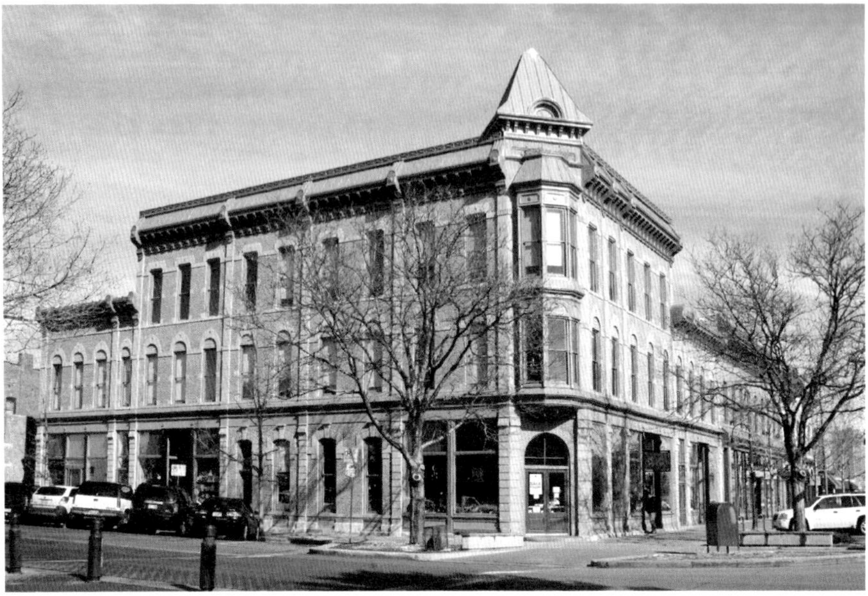

This building, designed as a bank by Montezuma Fuller, features a façade of pink sandstone from the quarry at Stout. *Photographed by and courtesy of Malcolm McNeill.*

paved streets (still wide in Old Town) handle a large volume of traffic every day. The women of the WCTU would be astonished to see bars and taverns in Old Town and elsewhere, for the dry times have come and gone.

The sugar beet factory that employed so many people and brought diversity to the community has been closed for decades, replaced by other industries, some of them quite high tech. The high school hailed as a sign of progress in the 1880s has been supplanted by four high schools that serve an ever-growing population. The new corporate headquarters of Woodward is being built on land once homesteaded by John and Emily Coy, preserving the barn that Coy built over one hundred years ago.

The county hospital that served the ailing for so long has become Poudre Valley Hospital, part of University of Colorado Health, and the original building is gone, first engulfed by additions and finally razed for more renovations.

The train that residents cheered when it puffed into town in 1877 has become a source of controversy and concern—but trains still pass through town daily, no longer carrying passengers but bringing fuel, materials and other goods to wherever they are needed. It can safely be said that people no longer cheer as the trains roll by but might when the barricades lift and traffic can move again.

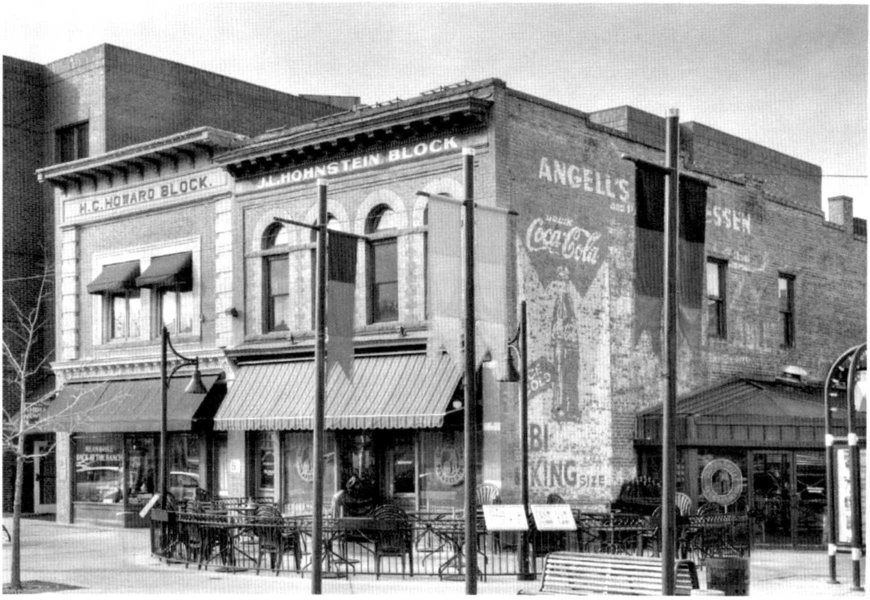

Local artist Barbara Moore chose this site to highlight one of several ghost signs still adorning buildings in Old Town. *Painted by and courtesy of Barbara Moore.*

Vestiges of the past remain, in downtown buildings that have been preserved (though many have been lost); in businesses that continue to thrive like the downtown Silver Grill, the longest continuously operating restaurant in Colorado; in the ghost signs that are still faintly visible on downtown buildings; and in the grace and beauty of houses built in another time, many of them still extant. Probably today's residents better appreciate the wide streets that so upset the long-skirted women when they were laid out.

The founders of this city would certainly not be surprised at the vagaries of nature—following several days of heavy rain, yet another flood wrought destruction, especially in nearby foothills, in September 2013. Memorable blizzards have come and gone, dealt with more efficiently than in times past but still causing disruption and destruction. Drought, fire and pestilence have plagued the land.

Yet surely the forebears would be pleased at the tenacity and generosity of the people who live here. As much as the world has changed, inundated with technology, beset by political divides and myriad problems, the City of Fort Collins has kept a steady course toward a sustainable future in a livable community while grappling with population growth, environmental challenges and divisive issues. The university has pioneered research and graduated individuals who have contributed much to the betterment of humanity.

Even so, just as it was 150 years ago, all is not sweetness and light. The twenty-first-century residents of Fort Collins have problems to face and to solve, differences to address and troubling challenges to work through. They face a future far more complicated than did the original settlers.

The men and women who chose to stay in a small, isolated western outpost two centuries past would have much to marvel at, much advice to offer and considerable pride in the foundation that they built here. They would no doubt be surprised at some outcomes, pleased with others and concerned with some even as we are concerned today. Those who live here now, in turn, have so much to thank them for—their courage, their determination, their resilience, their sacrifices and, most of all, their faith in the small settlement they founded so many years ago.

Standing at the intersection of Linden and Jefferson Streets, one might easily call on the imagination and hear, on a sigh of the wind, the creak of a saddle, the whinny of a horse, the commanding voice of a soldier…Once, long ago, they were here.

Bibliography

Ahlbrandt, Arlene, and Mary Hagen. *Women to Remember of Northern Colorado.* Wellington, CO: Azure Publishing, 2001.

Bird, Isabella. *A Lady's Life in the Rocky Mountains*. Norman: University of Oklahoma Press, 1960.

Brinks, Rose. *History of the Bingham Hill Cemetery*. Laporte, CO: Rose Brinks, 1988.

Case, Stanley. *The Poudre: A Photo History*. Bellvue, CO: Stanley Case, 1995.

De Haes, John. *Partners in Power: A History of the Fort Collins Light and Power Utility.* Fort Collins, CO: City of Fort Collins, 1985.

Fleming, Barbara. *Fort Collins: A Pictorial History*. Virginia Beach, VA: Donning Company, 1985.

Fleming, Barbara, and Malcolm McNeill. *Then and Now Fort Collins.* Charleston, SC: Arcadia Publishing, 2010.

Fry, Norman. *Cache la Poudre, The River*. Poudre City, CO: Norman Fry Estate, 1954.

Gray, John. *Cavalry and Coaches*. Fort Collins, CO: Fort Collins Corral of Westerners, 1978.

Hansen, James. *Democracy's College in the Centennial State*. Fort Collins, CO: James Hansen, 1977.

Hensen, Dr. Stanley. *Touching Lives*. Fort Collins, CO: Stanley Hensen, 2005.

McLellan, Tom. *A History of the Fort Collins Police Department.* Bellvue, CO: Tomac Publishing, 2013.

McNeill, Malcolm. *The Automobile Comes to Fort Collins*. Fort Collins, CO: Malcolm McNeill, 2013.

Pennock, Iola. *Happy Hardships*. Fort Collins, CO: Iola Pennock, 1982.

Swanson, Evadene. *Fort Collins Yesterdays*. Fort Collins, CO: Evadene Swanson, 1975.

Sykes, Hope. *Second Hoeing.* Lincoln: University of Nebraska Press, 1935.

Tresner, Charlene. *Streets of Fort Collins*. Fort Collins, CO: McMillen Publishing Co., 1977.

Watrous, Ansel. *History of Larimer County*. Fort Collins, CO: Ansel Watrous, 1911, 1972.

Index

T

U

V

W

About the Author

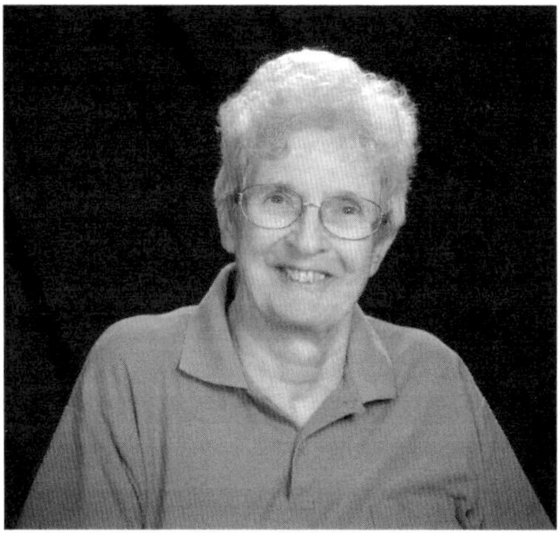

A native of Fort Collins, Barbara Fleming has lived there most of her life; the small college town in which she grew up has become a mid-sized city with a large university. She graduated from Colorado State University and worked as a teacher, then as a training coordinator, before retiring. She is the author of several books of local history and writes a weekly column on local history for the daily newspaper, the *Fort Collins Coloradoan*. An avid reader, she also enjoys spending time with family and friends, playing bridge and taking part in adult education classes. She has three grown children and two granddaughters and lives with her gray cat, Shadow.